FIGHTING THE
DESERT FOX

A Crusader of the Royal Gloucestershire Hussars passes a burning PzKpfw III, 28 November 1941. (IWM E6751)

FIGHTING THE DESERT FOX

Rommel's Campaigns in North Africa
April 1941 to August 1942

John Delaney

ARMS AND ARMOUR

ARMS & ARMOUR PRESS
An imprint of the Cassell Group
Wellington House, 125 Strand, London WC2R 0BB

Distributed in the USA by Sterling Publishing Co. Inc.,
387 Park Avenue South, New York, NY 10016-8810

British Library Cataloguing-in-Publication data:
A catalogue record for this book is available from the British Library.

ISBN 1 85409 407 6

Edited and designed by Roger Chesneau/DAG Publications Ltd

Printed and bound in Great Britain

CONTENTS

Introduction   7

1   Operation 'Sunflower'   9

2   Operation 'Brevity'   34

3   Operation 'Battleaxe'   36

4   Operation 'Crusader'   52

5   Operation 'Theseus'   84

6   Operation 'Venezia'   95

7   The Beginning of the End   129

    Index   157

INTRODUCTION

The fighting in North Africa between April 1941 and August 1942 holds a less prominent place in British military history than do the desert offensive of General Richard O'Connor in 1940–41 and the battles fought by General Bernard Montgomery from El Alamein to Tunis between October 1942 and May 1943. This is probably because these periods are characterised by significant Allied victories. The interval in between—upon which *Fighting the Desert Fox* focuses—shows the Allied Army in a much less flattering light.

The time frame considered here, April 1941 to August 1942, saw the darkest hours of the Allies' fortunes in North Africa: on several occasions it appeared that they were on the brink of defeat and expulsion from the Mediterranean coast of the continent altogether. With the notable exception of Operation 'Crusader', the period saw a succession of Allied battlefield defeats both in offence and defence. It also saw a series of British generals—Neame, Beresford-Pierse, Wavell, Cunningham, Ritchie and Auchinleck—all of whom faltered when confronted with the inspired tactics of Erwin Rommel, probably the finest battlefield commander to face the British during the Second World War.

The campaign in North Africa changed dramatically with the arrival in the Western Desert of Rommel and his famed *Deutsches Afrika Korps* (DAK). Instead of competing against a highly incompetent, inefficient and ineffective Italian High Command, the Allies found themselves up against the latest strategic and tactical concepts, carried through by a dynamic, aggressive leader. It took a long time for the British High Command to adapt and begin to cope with this new presence—time the Allies did not really have. Luckily for the British, the German High Command's decision to treat the North African theatre as a side-show, combined with Rommel's occasional lapses into over-confidence, led directly to massive logistical problems at the front that prevented the Axis army from finishing off its opponents. Finally, the British High Command found in Montgomery a general who could stand up to Rommel. (It is interesting to note, however, that Montgomery was the second choice to take command of the 8th Army behind Gott, an experienced desert campaigner but one imbued with all the preconceived ideas that adversely affected the decision-making of previous commanders.) Montgomery was a cautious general, completely different from Rommel in many ways, but his approach to desert warfare was sound, if unexciting, when compared to that of his opposite number. Using an attritional strategy, taking advantage of the superior Allied supply situation, he ground out a series of victories that eventually gave the Allies control of North Africa.

Before Montgomery arrived, and with him the primacy of logistic considerations on the desert battlefield, it was Rommel who caught the world's attention with his sweeping attacks and daring offensives, often made when significantly outnumbered and out-gunned. These thrusts nearly always brought battlefield victory for the *Afrika Korps*. It was just lucky for the Allies that the Axis failed to turn these victories into significant long-term strategic gains.

It is this period of manoeuvre warfare in the Western Desert—a period when swiftness of thought and action mattered more than deliberate planning and careful calculation—that I intend to examine in detail in the following chapters.

AUTHOR'S NOTE

Throughout *Fighting the Desert Fox* I have referred to the opposing armies as 'Axis' and 'Allied', except where I discuss specific formations or the various high commands involved. Thus, for example, I have examined the British High Command's policies but the Allied Army's movements. This is because major strategic decisions were inevitably taken by British officers, but the forces in the field were from a wide variety of countries, including India, South Africa, Australia and New Zealand (and non-Commonwealth countries such as France, Poland and Czechoslovakia). Some books on the desert war talk of British victories when in fact the price paid for that victory was the blood of soldiers from many nations. I do not wish to undervalue the significant contribution made by these countries to the war in the Western Desert. Likewise, many books talk of German achievements and ignore the major role played by the Italian Army in the desert campaign. Although there is a little truth in the assertion that some Italian units were far from trustworthy in battle, the vast majority of Italian soldiers fought bravely, being let down by inadequate equipment and poor leadership rather than by any lack of moral fibre.

ACKNOWLEDGEMENTS

I would like to thank all the staff of the Imperial War Museum Photograph Archive for their kind help and assistance, particularly Glyn Biesty, whose superb maps help bring to life the battles I have described. I would also like to thank my partner Helen: without her tireless efforts in proof-reading and re-typing my original manuscript this book would never have appeared. I must also pay tribute to the ceaseless encouragement I have received from my family and friends, who never flagged even when I did. Finally, my thanks go to Rod Dymott of Arms & Armour Press, who kept faith with me.

All the photographs appearing in this book are available on application from the Imperial War Museum Photograph Archive.

John Delaney

CHAPTER ONE

OPERATION 'SUNFLOWER'

After the disastrous defeat of the Italian Army in Libya at the hands of General Richard O'Connor's Western Desert Force during the winter of 1940/41, Hitler realised that to keep Italy in the war, and thus his southern Mediterranean flank free from interference, a *Sperrverband* (blocking force) of *Wehrmacht* troops was needed in North Africa. This would help stiffen Italian resolve and, it was hoped, halt the Army's retreat in Tripolitania. To lead this new force the *Führer* chose Lieutenant-General Erwin Rommel, an outstanding officer who had distinguished himself leading the 7th Panzer Division in the Battle of France. He had first come to Hitler's attention when he was chosen to command his personal bodyguard during the Polish Campaign.

The German force, consisting of the 5th Light (later 21st Panzer) and 15th Panzer Divisions, formed the heart of the new *Deutsches Afrika Korps* (DAK), which officially came into being on 19 February 1941. Exactly one week earlier Rommel had landed in North Africa to begin planning for the forthcoming campaign. Very few German units were present in theatre by the 19th. The 3rd Reconnaissance Battalion of the 5th Light Division had disembarked in Tripoli on 14 February. After being paraded through the streets of the town and inspected by General Italo

Gariboldi, technically Rommel's superior officer, they were despatched to the front line near Mugata on the Gulf of Sirte.

Over the next few weeks more units of the division landed at Tripoli. By 11 March the 8th Machine Gun Battalion, 606th Anti-Aircraft Battalion (equipped with 88mm guns), 39th and 605th Panzerjäger Battalions, 75th Motorised Artillery Regiment and the two tank battalions of the 5th Panzer Regiment were all present in Tripolitania. The Division's 104th Motorised Infantry Regiment did not arrive until DAK's first offensive was well under way. The first elements of the 15th Panzer Division did not begin to arrive in North Africa until the recapture of Cyrenaica was virtually complete.

Also placed under Rommel's command as part of DAK were the Italian Ariete Armoured and Trento Motorised Divisions (although called a motorised division this latter formation for the most part consisted of foot-slogging infantry). Both these formations were new to North Africa. Additionally, on 12 February Mussolini had authorised the temporary attachment of the Italian X Corps (Brescia and Pavia Infantry Divisions) to Rommel's command. These units, although hardened to the Lib-

Below: General Italo Gariboldi, with Rommel at his side, inspects men of the 3rd Reconnaissance Battalion, 5th Light Division, Tripoli, February 1941. (IWM HU5632)

Left, upper: Men of an anti-tank battery await their turn to parade through the streets of Tripoli to mark the arrival of the *Afrika Korps* to the theatre, early March 1941. (IWM HU70602)
Left, lower: The tanks of the 5th Panzer Regiment drawn up in a Tripoli side street, early March 1941. Note the preponderance of PzKpfw Is and IIs: only three PzKpfw IVs can be seen in the whole picture! (IWM HU70600)

spots. Campaigns, he felt, were not won by defensive postures, and the sooner he could begin an attack the safer the Axis position in North Africa would be.

It did not take Rommel long to realise that there was something wrong in the Allied camp. On his arrival he had been informed that the enemy force in Cyrenaica was at least an armoured corps and three infantry divisions strong. In fact it was nowhere near this strength. Rommel quickly persuaded Gariboldi to move his formations eastwards, and on 13 March, even as further German reinforcements arrived in Tripoli, he set up his headquarters at Sirte near the front line. The British position in Libya was in fact quite precarious, and, as Rommel was to show, all that was needed was a daring, rapid advance and the defences would collapse.

On the same day as that on which the new leader of the *Afrika Korps* landed in North Africa, the British command structure also underwent major changes. General Richard O'Connor returned to Cairo to become GOC (General Officer Commanding) Egypt, with General Sir Henry Maitland Wilson taking over as Military Governor and Commander-in-Chief Cyrenaica. This arrangement was itself short-lived, as Wilson was hurriedly shipped off to Greece after the British Mission there had reported on 22 February that Commonwealth troops were desperately

yan desert, were under-strength and woefully short of transport. They were to have severe difficulty keeping up with the offensive to come.

Allied propaganda sources were later to claim that the *Afrika Korps'* outstanding performance was in part due to their special training, and that their equipment had been specially adapted for desert conditions. None of this was true. All the German forces and a large proportion of the Italian units taking part in Rommel's first offensive were North African novices.

General Gariboldi was in favour of a defensive posture for the Italo-German Army, preferably pulled back from the present front line nearer Tripoli, and plentiful supplies. Italian forces were largely unmotorised, and becoming cut off far from a supply source had spelt disaster for the 10th Army the previous winter. Rommel was of a different caste of mind altogether. Always looking for a way to knock his opponent off balance, he advocated an aggressive forward defence, constantly probing the Allied positions and looking for weak

needed to shore up the Greek Army in the face of an almost certain German attack. For political and strategic reasons the Greeks could not be left to face the coming onslaught alone, and a large part of the Western Desert Force was withdrawn for the coming Balkan campaign.

Lieutenant-General Philip Neame (previously Commander-in-Chief Palestine) then took over Cyrenaica Command. Without a coherent corps structure in place—XIII Corps Headquarters had left for Egypt with O'Connor and its replacement, 1st Australian Corps Headquarters, had departed for Greece with Wilson—and with little time to reorganise before Rommel's attack, it is little wonder that from the very beginning of the campaign confused and often contradictory orders paralysed the British defensive effort.

As well as a shambolic command structure Neame inherited a much weakened Western Desert Force. The 7th Armoured Division, the spearhead of the forces deployed against the Italian 10th Army the previous winter, had returned to Egypt to refit and re-train. The 6th and 7th Australian Divisions, the New Zealand Division and an armoured brigade of the 2nd Armoured Division had all been redeployed to Greece. This left only the 9th Australian Division (commanded by Major-General L. J. Morshead), the remainder of the 2nd Armoured Division (the 3rd Armoured Brigade and a much reduced Support Group, under the command of Major-General M. D. Gambier Parry) and the 3rd Indian Motorised Brigade to defend the whole of Cyrenaica.

To make matters worse, the 9th Australian Division lost two of its three veteran brigades to Greece, the troops being replaced by green units recently arrived from Australia. The 2nd Armoured Division also had no desert combat experience, and its

commander had been in his post for less than two months. The 3rd Indian Motorised Brigade, although equipped with lorries (unlike the Australians, who had virtually no transport), had no artillery or anti-tank weapons at all. Instead, of the six artillery regiments normally attached to a formation of this size Neame was given three, one of which was equipped with First World War-vintage 18pdr guns. Instead of the two or three anti-tank battalions normally present, only one battery of 2pdr anti-tank guns could be found in the whole of Cyrenaica.

The 3rd Armoured Brigade was also in very bad shape. Although it consisted of three regiments, totalling nearly 200 tanks, it was in no condi-

Above: *Luftwaffe* **ground crew check and unload a camera from a Messerschmitt Bf 110 after its return from a reconnaissance mission. (IWM HU71018)**

tion to face a panzer force on the field of battle. Two-thirds of its vehicles were light tanks, unable to hold their own even against the PzKpfw II, one of the least capable German vehicles. The single regiment of medium cruiser tanks that the division did possess was plagued with mechanical problems, only 23 tanks being serviceable at the beginning of the campaign. To compound these problems there was a woeful lack of signalling equipment throughout the Western Desert Force. Not only were

Top and above: An Italian bomb disposal team at work on an unexploded British bomb which has fallen in a residential area of Tripoli. Although the RAF tried as best it could to limit damage to non-military targets, civilians were inevitably caught up in the attacks, handing Mussolini a propaganda tool which he used to the full. (IWM HU70618/HU70619)
Above centre: A column of PzKpfw II tanks on its way to the front passes through 'Marble Arch', a monument to Mussolini's African empire built on the Via Balbia in Tripolitania. (IWM STT467)

these units badly equipped to fight the *Afrika Korps*, they were badly informed as to what had to be done once the campaign was under way. The RAF had also decreased its forces allocated to Cyrenaica Command, three squadrons being sent to Greece. When Rommel's attack began only two fighter, one army co-operation and one light bomber squadron were available to aid the beleaguered Western Desert Force.

Because of the severe lack of transport in Cyrenaica Neame was forced to resupply his units from a series of static dumps dotted around the area, at Msus, Tecnis, Martuba, Mechili and Tmimi. This in turn tied his units to within a definite radius of these locations (because of this they were not able to occupy the defensible terrain west of El Agheila), undermining any flexibility of posture Neame might have had.

However, General Archibald Wavell as Commander in Chief Middle East estimated that Neame had at least until 16 April to prepare his defences. The British commander felt that it would need a minimum of

Above: The 'Desert Fox'. (IWM GER1281)

thirty days for Rommel to transport enough supplies to his forward areas to sustain even a limited offensive into Cyrenaica. It was likely that the German commander would wait until his main armoured force, the 15th Panzer Division, had fully disembarked. This would mean no major offensive until June, by which time Keren in Eritrea should have fallen, and at least one and possibly two Indian divisions, plus a South African division, would be available as reinforcements. Rommel had no intention of waiting that long, despite specific

orders given to him on 21 March which forbade an offensive to recapture Cyrenaica. Between the 17th and 23rd of the month he had been in Berlin putting forward a case for the deployment of two further German divisions to North Africa, arguing that with these forces he could evict the British from Egypt altogether. However, Hitler and Franz Halder, Chief of Staff of the German Army, were much more concerned with the coming campaign in Russia and told Rommel that Operation 'Sonnenblume' (Sunflower) was to be

nothing more than an aggressive defence of Tripolitania. The day after his return from Germany the DAK commander vigorously set about undermining the orders he had received.

As a preliminary to his thrust into Cyrenaica Rommel had first to clear the British garrison from the fort of El Agheila. This was achieved early in the morning of 24 March without a single German casualty. The King's

Dragoon Guards (the 2nd Armoured Division's reconnaissance regiment) pulled back to the much more defensible defile at Mersa el Brega, where the rest of the 2nd Armoured Division's Support Group were dug in. Before assaulting this next position Rommel carefully husbanded his forces and brought up supplies, the attack finally beginning at 8 a.m. on 31 March.

Under his command Rommel now had 37,000 Italian and 9,300 German troops—the *Deutsches Afrika Korps*, consisting of the 5th Light Division, the Ariete Armoured Division and the Trento Motorised Division; and the Italian X Corps, made up of the Brescia and Pavia Infantry Divisions. The main problems he faced in planning his attack were an acute shortage of motorised transport and a severe lack

of fuel for the vehicles he did possess, a logistical nightmare that was to return time and again in the campaigns to come. Because of this Rommel was forced to conduct his offensive in the main with only three divisions, the 5th Light (General Johannes Streich), the Ariete Armoured (General Ettore Baldasarre) and the Brescia Infantry (General Bartolo Zamboni).

The big guzzlers of precious petrol were of course the Axis armour, spearhead of Rommel's forces. When the assault began the Ariete had 46 M13 medium tanks and 117 CV33/ 35 tankettes operational. The 5th Light fielded a further 78 light tanks (PzKpfw I and II) and 80 medium tanks (PzKpfw III and IV). In direct support of these formations flew Fliegerkorps X, the *Luftwaffe* com-

mand in North Africa, commanded by Major-General Stefan Frohlich. This in April 1941 consisted of some 50 Ju 87 Stuka and 20 Bf 110 fighter-bomber aircraft. They were ably supported by the *Regia Aeronautica* (Italian Air Force), which added a further 90 fighters, 10 dive-bombers and 28 bombers to the total support aircraft available. They were able to dominate the air over Cyrenaica and provide Rommel with much-needed quick-response 'flying artillery'.

The first attacks against the Mersa el Brega position by the 3rd Reconnaissance Battalion of the 5th Light Division began at 8 a.m. on 31 March. Supported by artillery fire and Stuka dive-bombers, they quickly pushed back the defending British infantry, the 1st Battalion Tower Hamlets Rifles, from their trenches on Cemetery

Left: An SdKfz 251 half-track moves past the fort at El Agheila shortly after its capture, 24 March 1941. (IWM GER626)
Right, upper: PzKpfw III tanks of the 5th Panzer Regiment move up to the front prior to the launching of Operation 'Sunflower', March 1941. (IWM GER724)
Right, lower: Rommel chats to General Stefan Frohlich, head of the *Luftwaffe* in North Africa, before boarding his Fieseler Storch to return to the front. (IWM HU5590)

Hill, the only piece of high ground on the battlefield. With this position consolidated, tanks of the 5th Panzer Regiment moved forward and were engaged by 25pdr field guns of 104 Regiment Royal Horse Artillery, deployed behind the hill. The guns, firing over open sights, brought the advance to a halt. Probing attacks by German infantry and panzers continued throughout the morning, but the British infantry held firm at the base of the hill, ably supported by their RHA colleagues.

At 2 p.m. another attack was launched, this time with the support of several waves of Stuka dive-bombers, but still the British held their ground. Unfortunately for them Rommel had not been inactive during the morning. Sensing that the frontal assault was getting nowhere, he had earlier personally reconnoitred an attack route through the sand dunes along the coast which formed the northern flank of the British position.

At 4.30 p.m. Lieutenant-General Streich, at the head of a mixed *Kampfgruppe* of armour and infantry, launched an attack against the dunes. By dusk they had broken through and were in a position to roll up the British defensive line from the north. The British commander had already foreseen this and had earlier requested tank support from elements of the 6th RTR (6th Battalion Royal Tank Regiment) stationed near

the Via Balbia (coast road) some miles to the rear. However, this had been denied by Gambier Parry, commander of the 2nd Armoured Division, who did not want to see British armour committed to a night action. Because of this the British had no option but to abandon their defensive positions and fall back towards Agedabia. Rommel did not pursue, instead taking a brief respite during the night of 31 March/1 April to reconnoitre, bring forward more troops

and, more importantly, bring up more fuel.

The advance resumed in the morning of 2 April with DAK armour and motorised infantry forging on up the Via Balbia towards Agedabia, some sixty miles distant. Apart from stragglers overtaken and captured from the Mersa el Brega action, the only British troops encountered were a squadron of cruiser tanks of the 6th RTR (the vehicles requested on 31 March at Mersa el Brega) which sud-

denly emerged on the southern flank of the 5th Light Division, having been disguised beneath Bedouin tents. However, such a small number of tanks could not hold up the advance of a mechanised division for long: within minutes all that was left of the brave British rearguard was seven blazing tanks and five more vehicles 'in the bag'. By nightfall the main body of the 5th Light Division had established itself in Agedabia, with forward reconnaissance elements another 12 miles on up the coast.

Sensing that the British command had fallen into panic and disorder, Rommel now took a calculated gamble and split his force into three columns. If the British had possessed a cohesive formation of any size in the vicinity this dispersal of troops would have spelt disaster, but he had guessed correctly: the nearest Allied formation of any size was a brigade of the 9th Australian Division at Benghazi. The left-hand column of the three, consisting of the 3rd Reconnaissance Battalion and the Brescia Infantry Division, was ordered to push up the coast road to Soluch and Ghemines. In the centre a column of tanks and motorised troops, the bulk of the 5th Light and Ariete Armoured Divisions, under the command of Colonel Friedrich Olbrich (CO of the 5th Panzer Regiment), was to make for Antelat and Msus. On the right a totally motorised force, consisting of the reconnaissance battalion of the Ariete Division and the 8th Machine Gun Battalion, under the command of Colonel Graf

Left, upper: DAK infantry advancing on British positions at Mersa el Brega, 31 March 1941. (IWM MH5551)
Left, lower: Men of the 2nd Armoured Division's Support Group are questioned by a German officer after their capture at Mersa el Brega, 1 April 1941. (IWM MH5544)

von Schwerin, was to head with all speed across the neck of the Jebel Akhdar (the Cyrenaican peninsula containing both Benghazi and Derna) via Giof el Matar and Ben Gania. The remainder of DAK and the Italian X Corps were to follow the coast road and were already beginning to lag behind the main body of the advance because of a severe shortage of transport.

General Zamboni warned Rommel that the track to Giof el Matar was a 'death trap' and that the thrust to outflank the British and Australians could not work. To prove him wrong, Rommel, along with two aides, drove up the track, outpacing the head of Schwerin's column. It is fortunate that he did not take the Italian at his word, for the sweep through the deep desert was to bring spectacular results.

On his return to his new forward headquarters at Agedabia he was informed that the 5th Light Division's tanks had run out of fuel and that it would be another four days before the armoured advance could resume. Rommel ordered that every truck in the vicinity be stripped of its load (thus large quantities of food, spare parts and men were unceremoniously dumped by the roadside) and sent back to the fuel depot at Arco de

Right, top: A PzKpfw I of the 5th Light Division pushes on past destroyed British lorries and an abandoned camp near Mersa el Brega, 1/2 April 1941. (IWM MH5549)
Right, centre: A burnt-out A13 cruiser tank of the 3rd Armoured Brigade is used as a DAK observation post during Operation 'Sonnenblume', early April 1941. (IWM RML897)
Right, bottom: An A13 cruiser tank of the 3rd Armoured Brigade, 2nd Armoured Division, races forward to counter-attack German panzers during Operation 'Sunflower', 3 April 1941. (IWM E2629)

Fileni. He then gave General Streich 24 hours to get the division moving.

As there was to be no advance from the central column until 4 April, Rommel decided that he should visit the northern flank of his force and see what was happening. On arrival at the headquarters of the 3rd Reconnaissance Battalion he found that they had made swift progress and were rapidly closing on their objectives. An Italian priest who had struggled south against the tide of retreating British and Australians declared that Benghazi was in chaos and that Allied troops were beginning to evacuate the town. On hearing this Rommel immediately amended the coastal column's orders, telling them to push on with all speed to Benghazi.

Through his personal presence at the point of advance of each of his columns Rommel managed to maintain a momentum for the offensive that so easily could have been lost. It was this knack of being at the right place at the right time to see and grasp opportunities that made him such a formidable general. This restless energy and attacking spirit got

him into trouble even before the day was out. On returning to his Agedabia headquarters at the end of a long day with his troops in the desert, he was confronted by an angry General Gariboldi, who demanded to know what he was doing advancing past the objectives set him by his superiors (he had been told not to proceed past Agedabia) and why he had split his force so recklessly. Rommel lost his temper. Berating his Italian superior for not being able to see the great opportunity that had arisen, he refused to take any further orders from him. What could have been an inter-Axis crisis of the first order was fortuitously dissipated when a telegram arrived from the *Führer* congratulating Rommel on his success and giving him *carte blanche* to exploit the situation as he saw fit (the telegram mentioned that Mussolini also approved of his actions).

With his orders approved at the highest level, Rommel returned with renewed vigour to his plan for conquering Cyrenaica. He harried the supply officers of the 5th Light Division through the early hours of 4

Above: SdKfz 222 armoured cars on the road to Benghazi. (IWM MH5556)
Right, upper: Operation 'Sunflower', April 1941.
Right, lower: A column of Italian M13/40 tanks, led by a staff car and motorcycle despatch rider, on the move along a coast road. (IWM HU28386)

April to ensure that the tank advance could resume the next day. He also sent another order to the 3rd Reconnaissance Battalion telling them that when Benghazi had fallen they were to push east into the interior towards Mechili, leaving the Brescia Division to continue to push up the Via Balbia.

During the 24 hours that the Axis armour was halted, the British had a brief opportunity to regain their balance and put together a coherent plan for the defence of Cyrenaica. Unfortunately this chance was not taken. As soon as the Axis offensive began, Wavell (Commander-in-Chief Middle East) flew from Cairo with General Richard O'Connor, victor of the previous year's campaign against the Italian 10th Army. It was initially

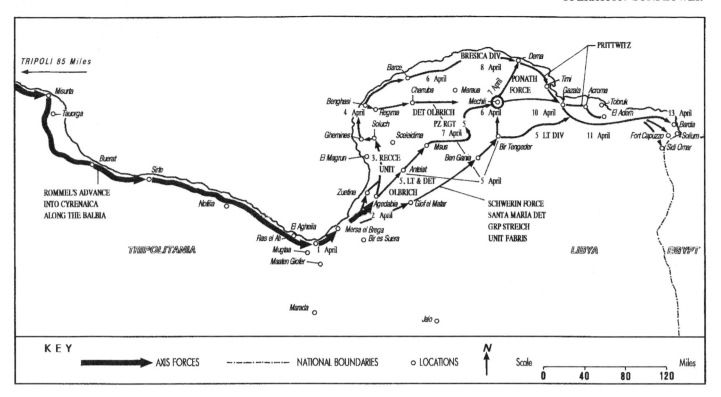

TRIPOLI 85 Miles

Misurta
Tauorga
Buerat
Sirte
Nofilia
El Agheila
Ras el Ali
Muqtaa
Maaten Giofer

ROMMEL'S ADVANCE
INTO CYRENAICA
ALONG THE BALBIA

TRIPOLITANIA

Marada

Jalo

1 April
Mersa el Brega
Bir es Suera
Zuetina
Agedabia
2 April
Giof el Matar
OLBRICH
5. LT & DET
OLBRICH
3. RECCE
UNIT
El Magrun
Ghemines
Sceleidima
Soluch
Regima
Benghasi
4 April
Charruba
6 April
Barce
Maraua
Mechili
DET OLBRICH
PZ RGT
7 April
Msus
Antelat
Ben Gania
5 April
Bir Tengeder
SCHWERIN FORCE
SANTA MARIA DET
GRP STREICH
UNIT FABRIS

BRESICA DIV
8 April
Derna
PONATH
FORCE
7 April
6 April
10 April
5 LT DIV
11 April

PRITTWITZ
Timi
Gazala
Acroma
Tobruk
El Adem
Fort Capuzzo
Sidi Omar
Bardia
Sollum
13 April

LIBYA

EGYPT

KEY ————▶ AXIS FORCES — · — · — NATIONAL BOUNDARIES ○ LOCATIONS N↑ Scale 0 40 80 120 Miles

Left: Italian Colonial Infantry man a Breda 12.7mm heavy machine gun, November/December 1941. (IWM MH9221)

his intention to replace Neame, a man with no desert combat experience, with O'Connor, a proven general. However, he seemed to change his mind when all three met on 2 April, possibly because O'Connor thought it unfair to deprive Neame of his command before he had had a chance to prove himself. Instead Neame would still be nominally in charge, with O'Connor acting as adviser. To add to this duality of command, Wavell himself was of the opinion that Rommel's offensive was limited and that Benghazi was his aim. He therefore ordered that measures be taken to prepare a defence of the town. Neame and O'Connor were convinced that Rommel would try to capture the whole of Cyrenaica and that concentrating forces at Benghazi would be playing into his hands. Thus a series of contradictory messages was sent from British Headquarters ordering units to do different things, often at the same time, by three different generals.

This appalling command system was mitigated somewhat by the even more terrible communications system the British had in place. For example, Wavell's order to concentrate at Benghazi was sent on 3 April but did

not arrive at the town until a day later, by which time it had become outflanked and untenable. The lamentable state of Allied communications meant that orders never arrived and consequently units were cut off and forced to surrender, or that orders arrived late and were out of date and consequently units moved in completely the wrong direction. Sometimes orders were plainly unrealistic.

The dispersed elements of the 2nd Armoured Division, dotted around south-western Cyrenaica, were ordered to retire to Mechili, where the unit would concentrate and be supported by the 3rd Indian Motorised Brigade (which was already there). However, the unit had not been provided with any tank transporters and consequently it had to travel everywhere under its own steam. Normally this would not have presented too much of a problem for an armoured division. However, the cruiser tanks were so mechanically unreliable that the brigadier in command of the 3rd Armoured Brigade estimated that if he withdrew across the 120 or so miles of desert as ordered he would reach Mechili with hardly any vehicles left, a trail of breakdowns in his

wake. Instead he ordered all of his troops that could do so to withdraw along the Via Balbia. This added to the already heavy congestion on the road caused by the withdrawal of other British and Australian units. Even with the more favourable rate of attrition obtained from travelling on tarmac, the 2nd Armoured Division reached Tobruk with precious few of its tanks (although much of its personnel got away). It was withdrawn from North Africa and never re-formed.

Things did not all go Rommel's way. At Regima, just east of Benghazi, the Australian rearguard delivered a sharp blow to the leading elements of the Axis advance. It was a minor victory , but one which nevertheless gave time to the withdrawing Allies and allowed more men to escape the noose that was soon to tighten around the Jebel Akhdar.

When on 4 April the armour of the 5th Light and Ariete Divisions wqas again ready to move, the lack of opposition being encountered by the southernmost column (Schwerin) encouraged Rommel to dissipate his forces yet further. Now the majority of the Ariete Division were to follow in Schwerin's tracks, leaving only 40 tanks with the central column. Rommel was thus strengthening the outermost reaches of his outflanking movement, confident that they could get through to the eastern end of the Jebel Akhdar and cut off substantial numbers of Allied troops. This Italian detachment was itself split into two columns, a mobile force of motorcyclists and light guns under the command of a Cornello Fabris in the lead, with the rest of the division following behind. Both columns were to follow Schwerin's forces up until Tengeder, where they would turn north to support the attack on Mechili if the 5th Light Division needed help, or turn east and head for Tobruk if the garrison had withdrawn. The 5th Light Division, minus its detachments but with Italian tank support, was to advance on Mechili via Antelat and Msus, as originally ordered. They would be joined by the 3rd Reconnaissance Battalion, who were even then pushing their way across the Jebel Heights towards Mechili from Benghazi.

Major-General Heinrich Kircheim, who was on a courtesy visit to North Africa, suddenly found himself placed in command of the Brescia Division for the next phase of operations. The division continued to push up the coast road, encountering periodic resistance from Australian rearguards. In its wake came the rest of DAK and the Italian X Corps, getting further behind the van of the advance every day. The British and Australians were unable to take advantage of the dispersal of the Axis forces, partly because they did not know where they were and partly because they had themselves been deployed too far away from each other to be of use. Thus the advance across the neck of the Cyrenaican peninsula became characterised by widely spread Axis columns, whose units knew their objectives, running across, fighting and capturing even more widely spread Allied units, who did not know where they were, what they should do or where they should go.

Throughout 5 April the advance continued, with Rommel observing the progress of each column from his own Storch light aircraft (he was a competent pilot). Occasionally, if a particular unit appeared to be in difficulties, heading in the wrong direction or stopped for no readily apparent reason, Rommel would land beside it to give instructions, chivvy it along or issue the relevant com-

mander with a severe tongue-lashing. This way he was able to monitor what was happening all across the front and keep his forces on the move. To his satisfaction, it soon became apparent that ever larger groups of British troops and tanks were becoming cut off, caught between the pincers of his advancing columns.

Being so involved at the front did have its disadvantages. Often, because Rommel could not be located quickly, important decisions had to be made by his staff back at Agedabia. Thus on 5 April his Chief of Operations, Major Ehlert, unable to contact Rommel, ordered Group Schwerin (8th Machine Gun Battalion, Ariete reconnaissance battalion) and the following Ariete detachments (Group Fabris and the main body of Ariete) to swing north at Tengeder, to attack Mechili from the south. Rommel, on his return to headquarters the next day, had to accept this manoeuvre, even though he wanted to push at least some of these columns eastwards towards El Adem.

Being so near the front also meant constant danger for Rommel. At any time his Storch could have been found and picked off by patrolling RAF fighter aircraft. He was also in danger from ground anti-aircraft and

small-arms fire, as he found out when he attempted to overfly an Italian unit on 8 April. The unit opened up at him with everything it had when he was only 300ft over the column. He managed to land nearby and gave the commander a good talking to, not so much because they had fired at him by mistake but because every single one of the hundreds of shots directed at him had missed the plane! There was also the danger of being captured by the British. This very nearly happened on 6 April when Rommel almost touched down next to a British unit, who had cunningly laid out a landing cross to entice him down. He realised his mistake just in time and managed to zoom away, rifle fire ringing in his ears.

Being out with the forward troops for great lengths of time also meant that Rommel could get delayed or lost, forcing him to spend the night in the desert, away from the nerve centre of DAK Headquarters. This happened on 5 April when, searching for the centre column (Olbrich), 5th Panzer Regiment and a detach-

Below: PzKpfw II tanks of the 5th Light Division move forward during Operation 'Sunflower', April 1941. (IWM GER624)

Above: Rommel, with his Chief of Staff Alfred Gause behind him, prepares to go aloft in his Fieseler Storch spotter plane. (IWM HU5635)
Below: Rommel observes enemy movements on a sector of the front held by the Ariete Division. An M13/40 medium tank of the formation provides the commander-in-chief with an armoured escort. (IWM HU60350)

ment of tanks from the Ariete, he strayed too far and was still out in the desert at dusk. Deciding to continue his hunt for Olbrich at night, he commandeered a car and set out across the desert. He found Olbrich's tanks at 3 a.m. after spotting some burning wreckage. Luckily he did not run over the patch of mines that he later found out was responsible for the vehicle's destruction. Unfortunately neither Rommel nor Olbrich now knew where they were. This could have spelt disaster for the whole operation—Rommel's main force of tanks and the commander-in-chief lost in the desert. However, luck was with Rommel and the pair were found at first light by two spotter planes, who relayed both their current position to them and the fact that Rommel was all right back to DAK Headquarters, one of the air-

craft landing to pick up the commander.

By 7.30 a.m. on 6 April a new set of instructions had been issued to the column commanders. The Fabris Group was to invest the southern approaches to Mechili, whilst the Schwerin Group were to swing round to the east of the town to block any escape in that direction. In addition, yet another column was to be created, this time from the 8th Machine Gun Battalion, part of Group Schwerin. Ten truckloads of infantry under the command of a Colonel Ponath were to head north from Mechili to the coast road (Via Balbia) near Derna. There they were to block the road to prevent any further retreat towards Tobruk by Allied forces; more troops would be sent to bolster Ponath's command when they became available. The 3rd Reconnaissance Battalion was to press on towards Mechili across the Jebel Heights, linking up with Group Olbrich (the 5th Light Division, including the 5th Panzer Regiment and a detachment of tanks from

the Ariete Division) advancing from Msus. They were then to proceed with all speed to Mechili to aid Group Fabris and Group Schwerin. The Brescia Infantry Division were to continue to harry the Australian rearguard and press on down the coast road towards Derna and Tobruk. As usual, the remainder of DAK and the Italian X Corps were to follow in their wake, well behind the combat zone.

Rommel was in favour of launching an immediate attack on Mechili with the Fabris and Schwerin battle groups, neither of which was above two battalions strong, but General Streich objected vehemently, arguing that more reinforcements were necessary before an attack could be contemplated, especially as they did not know exactly what Allied units were holed up in the fort and surrounding area. The arguments became somewhat academic when the Fabris Group reported that it had run out of petrol just short of Mechili and that because of this it was unable to deploy its light guns. Rommel, still

Above: Three Ju 87 Stukas pass over a DAK position after a successful bombing mission. (IWM MH5584)

hoping that a surprise attack could be launched quickly, set off personally to locate the required fuel. It took him several hours but he managed to gather together all the spare fuel belonging to Group Schwerin and Group Fabris, 35 cans in all, load them into a staff car and take them to Colonel Fabris's artillery.

The British force at Mechili, an old Turkish fort and oasis on a strategic desert crossroads, consisted of the 3rd Indian Motorised Brigade (minus one battalion), one battery of 104 Regiment Royal Horse Artillery (25pdr field guns), one battery of the 3rd Australian Anti-Tank Regiment (2pdr anti-tank guns) and the Headquarters section of the 2nd Armoured Division, all under the overall command of Major-General Gambier Parry. An attack against the fort was launched by Group Fabris very late

Right, upper: A 47-32 anti-tank gun of the Italian 8th Bersaglieri Regiment firing from the back of a truck. Both sides mounted and used guns in this manner. Called portees, these vehicle/gun combinations were able to shift position quickly, an advantage in the desert where a lack of cover and rock-hard ground made it impossible to hide or dig in. (IWM RML625)

Right, lower: General Philip Neame (left), General Richard O'Connor (centre) and Brigadier Coombe pause for a chat during a stop-over on their flight to Italy after their capture, April 1941. (IWM MH5554)

on 6 April but it did not fare well and it became apparent to Rommel that more troops would be needed to take the well-fortified position.

April 7 was a day of mixed fortunes for Rommel. It began well with a message in the early hours from Group Ponath that not only had they reached and cut the coast road west of Derna but they had also captured two British generals! The unfortunate capture of both General Richard O'Connor and General Philip Neame destroyed any hopes the Allies might have had of restoring the situation. Neame had spent most of 6 April searching for Gambier Parry in an attempt to ascertain what had happened to the 2nd Armoured Division. In fact Gambier Parry had already fallen back to Mechili to await the convergence of the formation there, but his message to Neame informing him of this had failed to get through. On returning to his forward headquarters at Maraua, where O'Connor was waiting, the decision was made that as the division could not be contacted the Western Desert Force HQ had better fall back along the coast road with the Australians. As O'Connor was only present in an advisory capacity he had not been allocated an official staff car. Neame therefore offered him a lift to Derna.

During the drive it became apparent that they had somehow veered off the main highway and were travelling along one of the minor roads running parallel with the Via Balbia. This did not seem to be a problem: they were miles behind their own lines and all the coastal roads led to Derna. Neame ordered his driver to carry on. Well after midnight their car was stopped by men of Group Ponath. The two British generals of Cyrenaica Command were 'in the bag'. Their capture was an incredible piece of luck for Rommel. Group Ponath was at this stage in no position to close the coast-

al highway to all traffic, only having ten truckloads of infantry. If Neame had kept to the main road, as most of the HQ vehicles did, he would have made it to Derna. Neame's second in command, Brigadier John Harding, was travelling on the same minor road, only 200yds in front of Neame's car, and he reached Derna without realising what had happened!

This promising start rapidly began to turn sour, however, when Rommel discovered that at first light on 7 April Group Olbrich could not be found. Group Fabris and Group Schwerin had manoeuvred themselves into position east and north of Mechili respectively, and the remainder of the Ariete Division (minus the tank detachment with Olbrich) was closing from the south. This left only the western approach to the fort uncovered. Rommel was counting on Olbrich to fill this gap and provide much-needed armoured support for the attack he wanted to launch that day. Rommel immediately took off in his Storch to scour the desert for the formation. Eventually, towards the end of the day, it was located well to the north of its intended route to Mechili, having been deflected from its course by a mirage. By the time the formation had been re-directed and had got under way it was too late to launch a full-scale attack on Mechili.

Luckily for Rommel, those inside the fort did not attempt to break out on 7 April. As far as they could determine, the Axis forces in the area consisted only of two small regiment-size battle-groups—not strong enough to take the fort or encourage an immediate withdrawal. In any case, they were still hoping for the arrival of armour from the 2nd Armoured Division, believed to be pulling back from Msus (although the decision to withdraw up the coast road instead of across the desert to Mechili never reached Gambier Parry). By first light on 8 April it became clear to Gambier Parry that further substantial Axis forces were moving on Mechili from the south (this was the bulk of the Ariete Division). There was no sign of the remainder of the 2nd Armoured Division, and so he reluctantly issued an order for his forces to break out and retreat to Tobruk.

The first sortie by the 3rd Indian Motorised Brigade began at 5.30 a.m. and attempted to force a passage through the troops defending the desert track to Tmimi. The 3rd Bersaglieri Motorcycle Battalion, part of

Above: Italian native troops man a Breda 20mm anti-aircraft gun. (IWM HU28380)

Group Fabris, supported by some 47mm anti-tank guns, beat off the attack after an hour of heavy fighting. The Indians then launched an attack northwards towards the tracks held by Group Schwerin and were similarly repulsed, although a small number of troops, including some Australians, managed to break through and escape.

Having been defeated in their attempts to break through on the direct routes back to British-held territory, the trapped Allied units then drove west down the desert track towards Msus. At first it seemed as though they might get away as no Axis troops seemed to be guarding the track. Indeed, if the lead elements of the column had been a little quicker they might have captured the German commander-in-chief!

As soon as the attempted Allied break-out began, Rommel took to the air to try to locate Olbrich's column, which had still not arrived on the battlefield. Unfortunately soon after take-off a sandstorm blew up west of Mechili which drastically reduced visibility. However, a stationary 88mm gun was spotted some two miles west of the town and Rommel, believing the gun to be in the van of Olbrich's advance, ordered the pilot to land next to it. As the Storch taxied to a halt it hit a sand dune, smashing its propeller. Worse news was to follow. The gun was not in fact with Group Olbrich but was on its own, having become separated from

the main column; not only that, but the weapon itself was disabled. It was at about this time that Rommel spotted a cloud of dust in the east—the 3rd Indian Motorised Brigade was heading in his direction! Luckily for Rommel, the crew of the gun possessed a truck that was in working condition and they were able to head away into the sandstorm to avoid being captured.

At roughly the same time the lead elements of Group Olbrich, the Headquarters Company of the 5th Panzer Regiment, emerged from the sandstorm to head off the Allied motorised column. Gambier Parry, mistaking the sandstorm for a dust cloud heralding the arrival of a very large mechanised force, ordered the col-

Left, upper: A Bersaglieri-crewed 47-32 anti-tank gun. This 47mm weapon was the mainstay of Italian anti-tank defence throughout the desert campaign, despite being of a relatively small calibre and possessing no gun shield to protect its crew. (IWM RML627)
Left, lower: Vehicles of the 8th Machine Gun Battalion in Derna, early April 1941. (IWM RML749)
Below: An 88mm gun being used in the anti-aircraft role by an Italian unit. Several '88s' were handed over to Italian formations to raise their fighting capabilities. (IWM STT2895)

umn to turn about. In fact the rest of Group Olbrich were some way behind and did not appear on the battlefield until the action was over.

The Allied force tried one last time to find an escape route, this time a gap between the southern flank of Group Fabris and the arriving Ariete Division. Unfortunately this southeastern thrust was too late, a significant portion of the Italian formation having already arrived on the battlefield. After being blocked by the 8th Bersaglieri Regiment, Gambier Parry ordered a surrender.

Rommel arrived back at a now Axis-held Mechili at noon to take the formal surrender of the British general and his troops. A further 1,200 men were now 'in the bag'. Group Schwerin and Group Olbrich (less the Italian tank detachment) were not given any respite after the victory, being immediately despatched to Derna. The Ariete Division stayed on to garrison the fort.

Immediately after the ceremony Rommel left for Derna in his newly acquired 'Mammoth', an armoured command vehicle formerly belonging to Gambier Parry. He arrived in the coastal town at 6 p.m. to find that Group Ponath and the Brescia Division had successfully linked up with Schwerin's and Olbrich's forces. Also waiting to meet him was Major-Gen-

eral Heinrich Prittwitz und Gaffron, the commander of the 15th Panzer Division, who had arrived with the lead elements of the formation in Tripoli a few days earlier.

The ever-restless Rommel quickly found work for the new commander. Prittwitz was given command of the 3rd Reconnaissance Battalion, the 8th Machine Gun Battalion and the 605th Panzerjäger Battalion and told to pursue the retreating Australians down the coast road to Tobruk. The rest of the 5th Light Division was to wheel south, then east, through the desert and block the coast road between Bardia and Tobruk. The garrison was to be sealed in by 11 April at the latest.

Rommel hoped that the Allies could be bounced out of Tobruk as they earlier had been forced out of Benghazi and Derna. If not, they would be encircled and destroyed as they had been at Mechili. Unfortunately for Rommel, Wavell had decided that Tobruk would be held at all costs—there was to be no further retreat. All possible reinforcements that could be found had been fed into the port, supporting the Australians already there who had retreated from Cyrenaica.

Neame had, over a month earlier, ordered further work to be carried out developing the already extensive Ital-

Above: A column of PzKpfw III tanks and SdKfz 222 armoured cars moves along the Via Balbia during the closing stages of Operation 'Sunflower', April 1941. (IWM HU39505)

ian-built fortifications around Tobruk, just in case the British had to retreat from Cyrenaica. Tobruk was a major supply base on the road from Egypt, it had a good harbour and its own airfields, and it was well fortified—a good defensive position for a siege. The last Australian units pulled back inside the town's perimeter defences on 9 April, the same day that Rommel's forces began their pursuit from Derna.

The largely Australian garrison of Tobruk was initially commanded by Major-General J. D. Lavarack (Lavarack, a corps commander was soon elevated to Commander-in-Chief Cyrenaica Command, the defence of Tobruk passing to Major-General Morshead). As well as the 20th, 24th and 26th Brigades of the 9th Australian Infantry Division, which Mors-

head had successfully evacuated from Cyrenaica, he now also had at his disposal the 18th Infantry Brigade (part of the 7th Australian Division recently returned from Greece) and the 18th Indian Cavalry Regiment (the only part of the 3rd Indian Motorised Brigade not to have been at Mechili). Armoured support consisted of a newly reconstituted 3rd Armoured Brigade, made up of survivors from the retreat and newly arrived vehicles. In total there were some 26 cruiser, 15 light and four Matilda tanks. Artillery support was provided by two Royal Artillery Field Regiments equipped with 25pdr guns and one Field Regiment equipped with twelve 4.5in howitzers and twelve 18pdr field guns. There were two anti-tank regiments (2pdr guns), each minus one battery. A total of 16 heavy and 59 light anti-aircraft guns provided cover against *Luftwaffe* and *Regia Aeronautica* attack. Many of these guns were Italian, captured during the previous year's offensive. In addition, the ever-resourceful Aus-

tralians brought out of store several dozen Italian field guns, also captured by O'Connor's force, and placed them in entrenchments around the Tobruk perimeter. Manned by infantrymen, they provided instant high-explosive fire support. Not to be outdone, the Australian cavalry regiment which provided the 9th Division's reconnaissance equipped itself with captured Italian M13/40 tanks (they had previously been armed with Bren Carriers). To identify themselves on the battlefield they painted large white kangaroos on the sides of their turrets.

On 10 April, as the German and Italian formations moved into position around Tobruk, DAK suffered its first and by no means its last general officer casualty. On reaching the perimeter defences of the town, General Prittwitz was ordered to attack with his meagre force of infantry and Marder tank destroyers. Rommel was hoping that the Allied troops would be so demoralised by their long retreat that the defences would collapse

Right: Tobruk 'Bush Artillery' in action, in this case a captured Italian 149mm howitzer. This particular gun was fired by the infantry by remote control, a 30ft long rope, the crew suspecting that the decrepit piece would explode when fired. (IWM E5535)

under the slightest assault. In this he was to be sorely disappointed, for the German probe was halted in its tracks, Prittwitz being killed by some very accurate anti-tank fire.

The tanks of Olbrich's 5th Panzer Regiment, having cut the road to Bardia on the 11th as instructed, were now joined by the remainder of the 5th Light Division, minus the 3rd Reconnaissance Battalion, which was detached to hold El Adem to the south of Tobruk. The Ariete Armoured Division had also moved up to El Adem to cover Rommel's right flank in case any British forces from Egypt attempted to interfere with the reduction of the town. General Zamboni's Brescia Infantry Division and General de Stefanis's Trento 'Motorised' Division deployed to the west of Tobruk, cutting the coast road to Derna and completing the envelopment of the port. By 14 April Axis force were in a position to launch a major assault on Tobruk.

The attack opened at 4.30 a.m., just after first light. The Trento and Brescia Divisions mounted small diversionary attacks to pin the defenders in position, while the main assault came from the 8th Machine Gun Battalion and the 5th Panzer Regiment of the 5th Light Division to the south of the town. The attack was a disaster.

The Germans totally underestimated the strength of the Australian defences and were soon bogged down

in a one-sided fire fight in the midst of the Allied position. The Australian infantry had cannily allowed the tanks of the 5th Panzer Regiment to pass through their first lines of defence, but had engaged and pinned down the following infantry much further back. This tactic was itself made possible by the heavy and very

accurate British artillery fire brought down on the panzers, forcing the infantry to follow them at a distance. The 5th Panzer Regiment, under heavy anti-tank fire from both flanks and now under direct fire from 25pdrs to their front, as well as a heavy indirect barrage, were soon forced to withdraw.

Right: A 25pdr field gun of the 1st Regiment Royal Horse Artillery fires on enemy positions outside Tobruk. (IWM E6561)

Above: The first PzKpfw IV to be captured by the British in the Second World War, Cyrenaica, April 1941. This tank was recovered from the battlefield and sent back to England for testing at the School of Tank Technology. (IWM HU62123)

Rommel, who had earlier left the battlefield to bring up elements of the Ariete Division to exploit the expected breakthrough, found on his return that the 8th Machine Gun Battalion was now on its own, surrounded by the enemy. He immediately ordered Olbrich to mount another attack, this time to extract Ponath's infantry. This second assault foundered almost on its start line, the tanks being able to make little progress against a concentrated hail of artillery fire. To make matters worse, the panzers came under attack from a squadron of RAF Blenheim bombers, causing further casualties.

No German troops were able to break through to the beleaguered 8th Machine Gun Battalion until it was almost dark, and by then it was too late. The battalion had suffered over 75 per cent losses, including 250 prisoners. Colonel Ponath, who had been awarded the Knight's Cross the previous day, was amongst those killed. The unit was effectively destroyed as a fighting force. The 5th Panzer Regiment had also suffered heavily, losing 16 out of 38 tanks committed to the attack.

Both Streich and Olbrich complained to Rommel that they had been given no idea of the depth and complexity of the Allied defences, and that without substantial reinforcements and accurate maps of the fortifications (the Italians had not at this point managed to find any diagrams detailing the defences they had themselves constructed) future attacks would not succeed. Rommel ignored his subordinates' advice. If German troops were incapable of capturing Tobruk, then perhaps his more numerous Italian allies would be able to.

The next attack was launched on 16 April by the Trento and Ariete Divisions and was more of a débâcle than the previous assault. The Italians, resigned to the fact that the attack was bound to fail (they had, after all, built most of the fortifications they were supposed to capture) put little effort into the assault. The attack was led by a regiment of the Trento Division that had never before seen combat. It had little artillery support, and the Ariete Division, who were supposed to be supporting them, turned up with only seven M13/40 tanks and twelve CV33/35 tankettes, after the attack had begun! The Italian infantry were easily dispersed by an accurate artillery barrage, which then shifted to their rear, stopping the Ariete's tanks from coming forward and the infantry from retreating. As soon as the units came under small-arms fire Rommel was treated to the humiliating spectacle of hundreds of Italian infantrymen throwing down their rifles and running towards the enemy trenches to surrender. The Italians were routed after suffering only 24 fatalities, over 400 infantrymen surrendering to the Australians.

Rommel was incensed by the poor performance of the Italians and demanded that they put in another assault the next day, obviously hoping for a better-planned attack. He was to be disappointed. General Baldassare, tasked with planning the attack, was as fatalistic as his brother officers. Instead of attempting an organised assault he called for volunteer tank crews to take part in a forlorn charge against the Australian positions. Eleven tanks took part. To add insult to injury the vehicles came under German as well as British anti-tank fire, *Wehrmacht* guns knocking out two of the attacking tanks!

Still Rommel did not give up. With the arrival of the lead elements of the 15th Panzer Division at Benghazi on 26 April he planned one more Italo-German attack on Tobruk. This was launched on the 30th, and although it failed to achieve the desired breakthrough it was markedly more successful than the previous attacks. Fresh German troops, along with elements of the Ariete Division, all under the command of a German, Major-General Heinrich Kirchheim (who had already successfully led the Italian Brescia Division), obtained a

Right: A German map of the defensive positions held by the Allies at Tobruk. The key translates as follows: Flugplatz = airfield; Forts, betoniert und modern ausgebaut = modern concrete fortifications for heavy guns; Kampfstande aus Beton = concrete gun emplacements; In Felsen = sangars (emplacements made from rocks); Pakstande = dug-in anti-tank guns; Panzerwehrgraben = anti-tank ditch; Drahtsperren = wire entanglements with mines; Minenfelder = minefields. (IWM MH5849)

lodgement in the south-western corner of the Tobruk defences which overlooked some of the town, a constant thorn in the defenders' side. No matter how hard they tried the Australians could not shift the Germans from this captured ground. The position was held until Tobruk was relieved.

Rommel wrote after the assault, 'It was now finally clear that there was no hope of doing anything against the enemy defences with the forces we had, largely because of the poor state of training and the useless equipment of the Italian forces. I decided to break off the attack until the arrival of more troops.' He could do little about the fatalism and pessimism of his Italian colleagues but he could act on his perceptions of his German commanders. Major-General Streich and Colonel Olbrich, both of whom were accused of not being aggressive enough in the field, were summarily dismissed from command.

While the fighting around Tobruk had been taking place a new front line had gradually established itself

just across the Egyptian border. For a while the only British forces holding this entire front were the tanks of the 11th Hussars. They were told to hold the 50-mile front through 'aggressive patrolling'. They did this so effectively that the German commander on the frontier reported that he was in danger of being cut off. This rather backfired on the Hussars as Rommel sent reinforcements which otherwise might never have appeared. However, these troops did not arrive until the British themselves had sent extra units to bolster the front line.

By the end of April the 11th Hussars had been joined by the 22nd Guards Brigade (2nd Battalion Scots Guards, 3rd Battalion Coldstream Guards, 1st Battalion Durham Light Infantry and 1st Battalion The Buffs). Initially the formation held the strategically important Halfaya Pass, whose heights overlooked the coast road from Sollum to Buq Buq, and through which ran the only other Libya–Egypt highway. Whoever held the pass was in a position to deny his

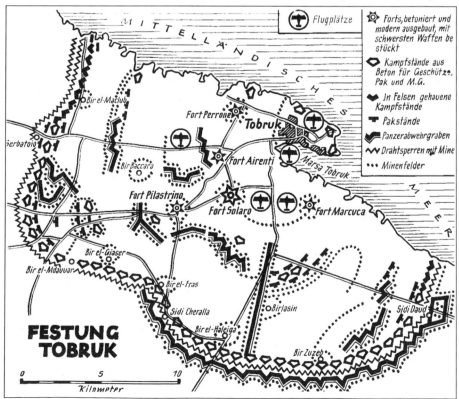

Above: Matildas on the move inside the Tobruk perimeter. (IWM E5558)

opponents the ability to make any significant advance to either the west or the east, possession of the road net being vital for supply convoys. At the top of the escarpment, where the road through the pass to the Libyan border entered the desert, a Free French infantry battalion was deployed, in a position that was to become known as Halfway House. The 2nd Battalion Rifle Brigade had also arrived at the front. This unit was split into four 'Jock Columns', each consisting of an infantry company, supported by a troop or two of 25pdrs and a few armoured cars or light tanks. Their role was to roam the interior south of Halfaya, watching for any enemy moves through the deep desert.

These fresh units—all new to desert fighting except for the Free French—had hardly settled into their new positions when they were hit hard by the significantly reinforced Kampfgruppe Herff, the mixed German and Italian formation tasked by Rommel to hold the frontier. Caught off balance, the British relinquished their hold on the Halfaya Heights and Halfway House, and were pushed back to all intents and purposes to the next main defensive position between Buq Buq and Sofafi. The Axis forces, content with the high ground, did not follow up. So the British still nominally held the terrain

Right: Italian troops receive instructions from a German officer mounted in a captured British truck; the DAK crew of another captured British vehicle, this time a Humber armoured car, look on. The Axis pressed hundreds of captured Allied vehicles of all types into service. This led to much battlefield confusion, but it enabled Rommel's forces to stay mobile. (IWM HU32688)

at the eastern end of the pass, and the road back to Buq Buq.

The recapture of Halfaya Pass was vital before any attempt could be made to mount a meaningful relief of besieged Tobruk. This was to be the number one priority of the new commander of the Western Desert Force, Lieutenant-General Sir Noel Beresford-Peirse. The British determination quickly to regain lost ground and open up a route to Tobruk led to the hastily planned and ill-conceived Operation 'Brevity'.

Right: A Free French captain consults his map and solar compass to check his position while out on patrol in the deep desert, 4 April 1942. Navigation across the featureless desert was a major problem for both sides in the North African campaign, and it was not unusual for whole divisions to lose their bearings and arrive late or completely miss a rendezvous with a sister formation. (IWM E10193)

CHAPTER TWO

OPERATION 'BREVITY'

Operation 'Brevity' was initiated because of the misinterpretation of two pieces of intelligence. First, 'Ultra', the top-secret code-breaking organisation based at Bletchley Park, England, had successfully intercepted and decoded messages sent back to Field Marshal Franz Halder from General Friedrich von Paulus. Halder, Chief of the German General Staff, had despatched von Paulus to North Africa specifically to prepare a dossier on Rommel, a report which might enable Halder, who disliked Rommel intensely (the feeling was mutual), to reign in this upstart of a general, who regularly ignored orders from his superiors. Von Paulus, a protégé of Halder, dutifully obliged and a series of messages highlighting (and over-emphasising) Rommel's sometimes cavalier approach to battle, the supply difficulties of DAK and the friction between Rommel and his Italian counterparts was sent back to Berlin. In addition, Middle East High Command had begun to receive reports that the new German formation just beginning to arrive in Tripoli was not, as had first been thought, another light division but was in fact a fully fledged panzer division. This would, thought Wavell, give Rommel another 400-plus tanks, and a decisive advantage in a desert encounter. What he did not know was that the standard panzer division organisation had been changed since 1940. Instead of two panzer regiments the 15th Panzer Division would now only contain one, the same as the 5th Light Division.

With these misleading pieces of information in his possession, and with continual pressure from Churchill to undertake some offensive action, Wavell thought that a pre-emptive strike against a disorganised and poorly supplied Axis force, before the arrival of a significant number of reinforcements which would make an offensive impossible, had a chance of success. He was wholly over-optimistic.

Operation 'Brevity' began at dawn on 15 May and lasted until the evening of the next day. It was an almost complete failure. Brigadier W. H. E. 'Strafer' Gott, who commanded the operation in the field, planned for a three-pronged advance against the Axis forces on the frontier. The 2nd Battalion Rifle Brigade, supported by 25pdr artillery fire, were to push up the coast road past the entrance to Halfaya Pass and take Sollum. They were then to force their way up the escarpment to capture the barracks at the top. The 22nd Guards Brigade, along with 24 Matilda tanks of the 4th Royal Tank Regiment, were to drive along the lip of the Halfaya Heights, capture the defensive position at Halfway House, where the road for Musaid and Fort Capuzzo exited the pass, and then push on to capture the fort itself. An understrength 7th Armoured Brigade

Below: British Guardsmen, supported by Royal Tank Regiment Matildas, move forward through a dust storm. (IWM E13940)

Above: A DAK PzKpfw III on the move. (IWM HU32679)

Group, containing 29 cruiser tanks of the 2nd and 6th RTR and the 1st Battalion King's Royal Rifle Corps, was to sweep round the Axis defensive positions via Sidi Suleiman, the Hafid Ridge and Sidi Azeiz, to be in a position to exploit towards Bardia and Tobruk. If the morale of Rommel's troops was as low as expected, his command in such a dysfunctional state and his supplies as precarious as intelligence foretold, then the defence should crumble quickly and the road to Tobruk be left open.

Unfortunately for Gott, Rommel and his men were not aware of their predicament and the projected collapse just did not happen. After a hard day's fighting The Rifle Brigade had managed to capture Sollum but had had no success in gaining the heights beyond. The 22nd Guards Brigade had fared a little better, taking Halfaya Pass and pushing on steadily towards Fort Capuzzo. The Armoured Brigade Group had swept out into the desert as ordered and were moving on Sidi Azeiz.

May 16 saw a steady reversal of fortunes for the British. After an ini-

tial success, when the 1st Battalion Durham Light Infantry managed to capture Fort Capuzzo, things went badly wrong. The 2nd Battalion Rifle Brigade got nowhere in its attempt to force a way into Sollum Barracks, whilst the 7th Armoured Brigade Group came under increasing enemy pressure in the Sidi Azeiz area. When a German *ad hoc* formation, Kampfgruppe Herff, headed by the 8th Panzer Regiment, forced the 22nd Guards Brigade to retreat first to Musaid and then back towards Halfaya, Gott realised that the expected pushover was not going to materialise, and that the small number of

units under his command were not going to be enough to hold on to his gains, let alone open up a route to Tobruk.

At 11 p.m., worried that the continued inroads into the centre of the British position would lead to the 7th Armoured Brigade Group's becoming cut off deep inside enemy territory, Gott ordered a general withdrawal to defensive positions at Halfaya Pass, hoping to hold on to at least some of the territory captured in the offensive. The Germans, satisfied that their fierce defence and early counter-attack had blunted the British offensive, were satisfied to leave the British in possession of Halfaya Pass—temporarily.

Ten days later, on 26 May, Kampfgruppe Herff launched an attack on the newly acquired British positions. Within 24 hours they had been forced back to their pre-'Brevity' start line. British losses for the operation amounted to some 333 men and five Matilda tanks. The Germans took 258 casualties, whilst the Italians lost 395 men.

Below: Two LRDG (Long Range Desert Group) patrols meet up in the deep desert, 25 May 1942. (IWM E12390)

CHAPTER THREE

OPERATION 'BATTLEAXE'

Wavell began to plan for 'Battleaxe' as soon as Rommel's advance had come to a halt, but he had been persuaded to try a much smaller offensive, 'Brevity', because of the information he had received on German present and future combat capabilities. As soon as 'Brevity' was over Wavell came under pressure to mount another offensive to relieve Tobruk, for both political and military reasons.

The capture of Crete by German paratroopers (the island had fallen on 31 May) meant that Axis forces in Cyrenaica could now be resupplied from shipping sailing down the western coast of Greece via the island. To enable the RAF effectively to inter-dict this and other supply routes to Tripoli, air bases between Sollum and Derna would need to be recaptured. The loss of Crete was yet another blow to British prestige, and to the political reputation of Winston Churchill in particular. A victory was desperately needed: it would lift morale back home and secure Churchill's hold on the post of Prime Minister. Churchill was also worried about the effect the loss of Tobruk would have on Anglo-Australian relations should the largely Australian garrison be overrun.

Wavell issued his main orders for the forthcoming offensive on 28 May. The Western Desert Force would recapture the Halfaya Pass and secure the Bardia–Sollum–Fort Capuzzo road net. The main enemy force was to be defeated in the desert between Tobruk and El Adem, then Allied troops were to push on and secure Derna and Mechili. The Tobruk garrison would sally forth to the south of the town, both to tie down significant numbers of Axis troops and, it was hoped, to punch a hole in the siege lines through which the port could be relieved.

Wavell set 15 June as the date for the opening of the attack, despite Churchill's urging him to strike earlier. The main problem he faced was that the 7th Armoured Division, the main armoured formation then in North Africa, had been largely dispersed in February and it would take time to reconstitute and retrain with the tanks recently received from Britain. The 'Tiger' convoy, which Churchill had bravely ordered to sail straight to Egypt via the Mediterranean, rather than follow the much longer route via South Africa, had supplied Wavell with 82 cruiser, 21 light and 135 Matilda tanks, all of which were desperately needed.

The Germans had also been building up their strength. The 15th Panzer Division, now commanded by General Freiherr von Esebeck, had

Left: An SdKfz 263 Panzerfunk-wagen of DAK Headquarters on the Via Balbia, June 1941. (IWM RML755)

fully disembarked, and Rommel placed it on the frontier in support of the Italian infantry already dug in there. As well as the Trento Division (61st and 62nd Infantry Regiments, 7th Bersaglieri Regiment, 46th Artillery Regiment and 551st Anti-Tank Battalion), he now had the tanks of the 8th Panzer Regiment, the field guns of the 33rd Artillery Regiment and the infantry of the 104th and 115th Rifle Regiments to bolster his front-line strength. Rommel withdrew the battered 5th Light Division from the front line and moved it into reserve. To combat the RAF in the coming battle he could rely on a total of 84 bombers and 130 fighters (German and Italian aircraft).

Available for the assault on the Axis positions was a reconstituted XIII Corps made up of the 7th Armoured Division, commanded by Major-General Michael Creagh. The division was made up of the 4th Armoured Brigade (4th and 7th RTR) and the 7th Armoured Brigade (2nd and 6th RTR). The 11th Hussars provided divisional reconnaissance, while the formation's Support Group consisted of four batteries of Royal Horse Artillery (25pdrs) plus the 1st Battalion King's Royal Rifle Corps and 2nd Battalion Rifle Brigade.

Wavell also had available the 11th Infantry Brigade of the 4th Indian Division (2nd Battalion Cameron Highlanders, 1st/6th Rajputana Rifles and 2nd/5th Mahrattas) and the 22nd Guards Brigade, so recently pushed back from the pass—all commanded by Major-General Frank Messervy. The RAF provided 105 bombers for ground support duties—more than the *Luftwaffe* and *Regia Aeronautica* combined—but only 84 fighters were available to fend off Axis aircraft, and the fight for air superiority over the battlefield was to be finely balanced.

The final plan envisaged the 22nd Guards Brigade, the 11th Infantry Brigade and the 4th Armoured Brigade assaulting and capturing the Halfaya Heights, then pushing on to take Fort Capuzzo, Sollum and Bardia. Meanwhile the 7th Armoured Brigade and the 7th Armoured Division Support Group were to sweep through the desert in an arc, taking in Sidi Omar, Hafid Ridge (an area of high ground west of Fort Capuzzo) and Sidi Azeiz. They would then be in a position to strike down the Via Balbia to Tobruk. They would also have trapped any remaining Axis troops on the frontier between themselves and Messervy's command.

Beresford-Peirse realised that Rommel was bound to react swiftly to the offensive and foresaw the 7th Armoured Brigade engaging the armour of the 15th Panzer Division in an encounter battle somewhere along its route of advance. Each side had roughly equal numbers of tanks, and the battle would be even. However, Beresford-Peirse felt that the capture of Halfaya Pass would not be difficult (it had not taken Rommel very long) and that the 4th Armoured Brigade would be released in time to come to the aid of the remainder of the 7th Armoured Division before the situation became critical. In this premise he was badly mistaken. Beresford-Peirse both underestimated Rommel and overestimated the fighting qualities of his own troops. The Axis commander reacted with admirable speed to the British offensive, realising immediately that it was not a raid or a feint but a ma-

Below left: A Stuka in *Regia Aeronautica* service undergoes an overhaul. (IWM HU70999)
Below right: Leutnant Hans Joachim Marseille, the highest-scoring *Luftwaffe* ace of the desert campaign, stands next to his 30th kill, an RAF Hurricane, March 1942. (IWM HU40167)

jor thrust. Within hours of the attack beginning, the 5th Light Division was motoring towards the frontier.

Not only were significant German reinforcements to arrive on the battlefield well before they were expected by the British, they were not deployed as anticipated either. Instead of feeding them into the Axis defensive positions on or near the frontier, Rommel decided to turn the battle to his advantage by initiating his own outflanking manoeuvre. The 5th Light Division were ordered to move on Sidi Omar, outflank the 7th Armoured Brigade and roll up the British line.

To make matters worse, the swiftness of the Axis response was mirrored by a stuttering start to the offensive by the British. The opening attack by the 11th Infantry Brigade on the Halfaya Heights was a dismal failure. The two Indian battalions of the brigade, supported by six Matilda tanks of A Squadron 4th RTR, who had been assigned the task of clearing the bottom of the pass, ran headlong into Italo-German defensive po-

Below: An Italian Breda 20mm 65 anti-aircraft gun being used in a ground role. (IWM RML618)

sitions commanded by the Reverend Major Wilhelm Bach. Within minutes all six tanks had been knocked out and the Indian troops pinned down at the entrance to the pass. It is interesting to note that the British claimed that the tanks were lost as a result of running into an extensive belt of mines, whilst the Italians argued that anti-tank gun fire from emplaced 47mm guns, directed against the tracks of the Matildas, was what brought the armoured advance to a halt.

Along the lip of the escarpment advanced the 2nd Battalion Cameron

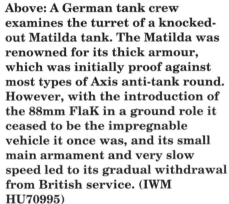

Above: A German tank crew examines the turret of a knocked-out Matilda tank. The Matilda was renowned for its thick armour, which was initially proof against most types of Axis anti-tank round. However, with the introduction of the 88mm FlaK in a ground role it ceased to be the impregnable vehicle it once was, and its small main armament and very slow speed led to its gradual withdrawal from British service. (IWM HU70995)

Highlanders, accompanied by 13 more Matildas. Their objective was to capture Halfway House, the defensive position at the top of the pass. They, too, ran into trouble. The attack began badly, with the artillery barrage planned to cover the assault never beginning because the artillery tractors following in the wake of the infantry became bogged down in a large expanse of soft sand. Halfway House, another of Bach's positions, was defended by a battery of four 88mm guns, along with a mixed force of German and Italian infantry. The German artillery, with an effective range far greater than that of the 2pdr guns on the infantry tanks, tore into the advancing armour, only one tank surviving the concentrated fire. The Matilda, its armour proof against Italian anti-tank guns at all but point blank range, was no longer the impregnable queen of the battlefield.

The German infantry immediately counter-attacked and the Highlanders were soon forced to retreat into the cragged wadis along the edge of the escarpment. Here they remained, pinned down and unable to do anything other than watch the Indian battalions' attacks falter far below in the valley floor. The 22nd Guards Brigade, accompanied by the Matildas of the 7th RTR (the 4th Armoured Brigade was equipped entirely with these very slow infantry tanks) manoeuvred to the south of the pass, outflanking Bach's defensive positions, and headed straight for Fort Capuzzo, some ten miles to the rear. This they took with surprising ease, the garrison melting away into the desert north of the fort. The Guards Brigade did not realise it but the

Germans had fallen back on the main body of the 15th Panzer Division, held in reserve between them and Bardia.

This fairly spectacular advance had only been achieved through the efforts of the remainder of the 4th RTR, along with infantry detached from the Guards Brigade who had entered into a fierce battle for Point 206, a heavily fortified desert hillock directly south of Fort Capuzzo and due west of the Halfaya Pass. The motorised infantry of the Guards had passed by this position within artillery range but they had not been fired upon, the defenders being too busy fighting off the advancing Matildas. The hillock changed hands twice during the day's fighting and was only secured at dusk with the arrival of B Squadron 4th RTR, fresh to the battle, eight Matildas having been lost

to close-range German 37mm and 50mm anti-tank fire.

The 7th Armoured Brigade appeared, at least initially, to be doing very well with its wide sweep around the Axis defence line. The brigade was led by the 2nd RTR, who were equipped with A9, A10 and A13 cruiser tanks, whilst the following 6th RTR were equipped entirely with the new Crusader cruiser tank. These vehicles were kept to the rear for possible use a pursuit force. The tank, capable of 27mph, was the fastest on the British inventory, and it was hoped that the new design would come as a nasty surprise to the Axis troops.

By 9 a.m. the lead elements of the brigade had reached the Hafid Ridge,

Below: Operation 'Battleaxe', 15–17 June 1941.

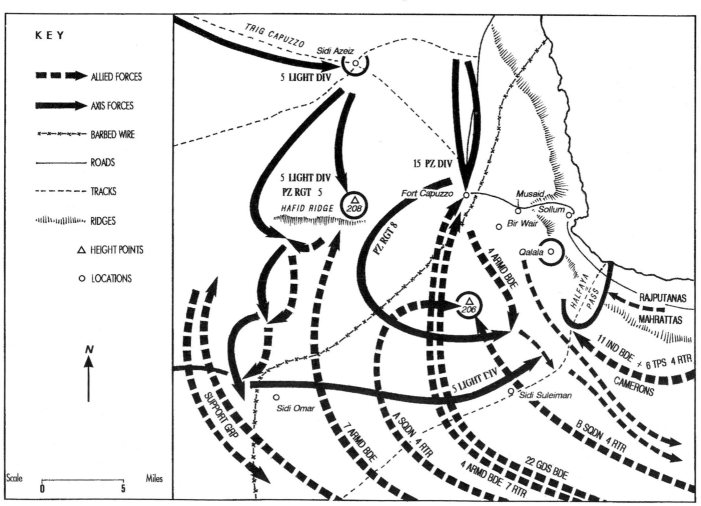

Above: A Crusader tank on the move. (IWM E14426)

an area of high ground approximately eight miles west of Fort Capuzzo. If they could capture the ridge the 7th Armoured Brigade would be in an excellent position to exploit the open country beyond, perhaps cutting off all the German units near the frontier from their El Adem and Derna supply sources—or so they thought. It had not yet been realised that the 5th Light Division, now commanded by General Johann von Ravenstein, had already reached Sidi Azeiz, some ten miles to the north of the ridge. The tactical options arising from the capture of the ridge were, however, never to worry the 7th Armoured Brigade commanders because it was on Hafid Ridge that the already faltering Operation 'Battleaxe' was to flounder.

Hafid Ridge in fact consisted of not one but three gently sloping rises, one

behind the other. Deployed between the first two crests was part of the German 1st Oasis Company, along with some Italians and a few 37mm anti-tank guns. Towards the eastern end of the ridge lay Point 208, an old Arab graveyard. This now heavily fortified position was the highest point on the battlefield. Not only did it overlook the three crest lines but it effectively enfiladed the valleys between. Defending this position were the rest of the 1st Oasis Company, with four 88mm guns attached.

With commendable patience the 88mm gunners let the tanks of the lead squadron of the 2nd RTR advance up and over the crest of the first ridge. As soon as they reached the top they were met with a hail of fire from the dug-in infantry and guns in the valley below. At this short range even

Right: DAK infantry man their foxholes on the front line. (IWM HU32770)

37mm anti-tank guns were effective and two A9 cruisers were quickly knocked out; the rest of the squadron turned tail and retreated back down the slope whence they had come.

The commander of the 2nd RTR was faced with a significant problem. His cruisers, armed with 2pdr guns, did not have the ability to fire high-explosive shells. This was no disadvantage in a tank-versus-tank engagement but it meant that it would be almost impossible to shift infantry in trenches and dug-in anti-tank guns. The few field guns that had been attached to the 7th Armoured Brigade were well to the rear, behind the 6th RTR. The vast majority of the 7th Armoured Division's 25pdrs were even further away, with the Support Group in the deep desert to the southwest, covering the left flank of the advance. He decided that a full frontal attack was not an option. Instead, a squadron of A9 and A10 cruisers was sent on an outflanking manoeuvre to the western end of the heights. The vehicles were then ordered to turn into the first valley and attack

Left: General Walther Neumann-Sylkow, commander of the 15th Panzer Division (second from right), explains a plan of attack to his regimental commanders. (IWM HU5609)

the German position from the flank. Meanwhile the rest of the regiment would wait for tank and artillery reinforcements.

The flank advance by the cruisers initially went very well. The attack caught the Germans by surprise and the tanks were able to move along the enemy trench line, strafing infantry and gun positions from close range. As they neared the eastern end of the defences they had only lost one vehicle to enemy fire. It was at this point that the squadron commander became aware of the defensive positions on Point 208, and he immediately ordered his unit to retire over the ridge. Unfortunately, owing to a shortage of radios (which meant that the squadron possessed only one set for every four tanks), five vehicles failed to respond immediately. They trundled on towards the eastern end of the heights and all of them were destroyed by emplaced 88s.

Things then went from bad to worse for the 7th Armoured Brigade. As the 2nd and 6th RTRs and their supporting artillery manoeuvred into position for a combined assault on the ridge line, news was received from RAF reconnaissance aircraft that German armour (the 5th Panzer

Regiment of the 5th Light Division) had been detected to the north. The 7th Armoured Brigade were going to have to clear Hafid Ridge of enemy quickly, if they were to use the heights to obtain a hull-down fire advantage over the approaching panzers. However, there were encouraging signs. Forward observers reported that the infantry and anti-tank guns in the first valley appeared to be preparing to pull out. Brigadier H. E. Russell, in command of the 7th Armoured Brigade, immediately ordered the Crusaders of the 6th RTR forward. As hoped, on topping the first rise they saw trucks and guns disappearing over the crest line opposite. Perhaps the machine-gunning they had received had broken their resolve. The Crusaders sped into pursuit.

Unfortunately, this is not what had happened. On topping the second rise the tanks ran into a hastily assembled gun line. The 88s from Point 208 joined in the fire fight, enfilading the second crest line, and Hafid Ridge was soon littered with burning British tanks. The German 37mm anti-tank guns and infantry, without the benefit of trenches and dug-outs, also took heavy casualties,

but the tide was turned with the arrival on the third ridge of the leading tanks of the 5th Panzer Regiment. The 7th Armoured Brigade disengaged and began to fall back towards the frontier at dusk on 15 June.

The 15th Panzer Division (General Walther Neumann-Sylkow) had spent the day skirmishing with the 22nd Guards Brigade and 7th RTR at Fort Capuzzo. With orders not to become fully engaged, Neumann-Sylkow had used a few of his tanks to try to lure British forces away from the fort. By pretending to fall back in disorder before the Matildas, the Germans found it relatively easy to tempt the British tank commanders into a rash pursuit, where they fell foul of well-concealed German anti-tank guns further to the rear. However, the fighting was not too heavy, the Guards held on to Fort Capuzzo with relative ease and the 7th RTR only lost a half dozen Matildas to enemy fire.

So, after the first day's fighting the 11th Infantry Brigade had failed to take Halfaya Pass and the 7th Armoured Brigade had been repulsed from Hafid Ridge. The only good news for the British was that the 22nd Guards Brigade had obtained a firm lodgement in the centre of the Axis position at Fort Capuzzo. However, Beresford-Peirse still felt that he could turn the situation round. That night he ordered the 11th Infantry Brigade to renew its attack on Halfaya Pass and the 22nd Guards Brigade to hold its ground. The 7th Armoured Brigade would be reinforced by the hitherto dispersed Matildas of the 4th Armoured Brigade. The mass of armour would then

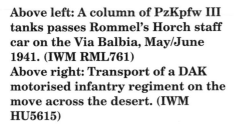

Above left: A column of PzKpfw III tanks passes Rommel's Horch staff car on the Via Balbia, May/June 1941. (IWM RML761)
Above right: Transport of a DAK motorised infantry regiment on the move across the desert. (IWM HU5615)

seek a tank battle with the outnumbered panzers of the 5th Light Division, the Axis would be defeated and once more a route to Tobruk would be open.

Rommel had no intention of fighting a set-piece armoured engagement. He did not believe that the principal role of tanks was to engage and destroy enemy armour. German panzer tactics were based firmly on the 'theory of the indirect approach' which underpinned Blitzkrieg. Armour's role on the battlefield was to seek out the weak spots in the enemy line, usually infantry positions, break through them and move with all possible speed into his rear areas, to cut lines of communication and sow the seeds of panic and disorder. His response to 'Battleaxe' would follow this doctrine.

The 5th Light Division were ordered on no account to become bogged down in a battle of attrition with the 7th Armoured Brigade. Instead it was to swing south as quickly as possible towards Sidi Omar, passing wide of the left flank of the British armour. The panzers were then to push east, then north, to reach the cut-off de-

fenders of Halfaya Pass and encircle and entrap the majority of the attacking British west of the frontier.

The best way for the 15th Panzer Division to support this move would be to try to pin the 22nd Guards Brigade in position and not allow them to withdraw. Rommel therefore ordered Neumann-Sylkow to undertake a determined attack against Fort Capuzzo. In addition to stopping any withdrawal it was hoped that the pressure applied by the panzers would delay the transfer of the 4th

Armoured Brigade to the support of Brigadier Russell and his men.

The advance of the 15th Panzer Division began at 5 a.m. on 16 June and battle was joined about an hour later. The previous day the garrison of the fort had managed to capture the nearby village of Musaid, and the brunt of the first thrust landed there. However, the Guards, in strong defensive positions, held on effectively. The British troops, thoroughly trained for positional warfare and well supported by 25pdr field guns

brought up during the night, saw off the fierce assault, causing considerable casualties. In a very bloody fire fight lasting four hours Neumann-Sylkow lost 50 of the 80 panzers he had committed to the attack. The only bonus for Rommel was that the Matilda tanks of the 7th RTR were fully engaged beating off the assault and were thus unable to move to the British left flank.

By midday the 15th Panzer Division had had enough. Neumann-Sylkow ordered the withdrawal of the formation, salvaging whatever he could from the battlefield. The Guards Brigade waited, sure that, once the Germans had reorganised, they would try again. Indeed, to strengthen their defensive position the 2nd Battalion Scots Guards pushed east to capture Sollum Barracks, thus preventing the Axis from turning the right flank of the defenders or reaching Halfaya Pass. However, the 15th Panzer Division did not launch any further frontal assaults—

Left: General Walther Neumann-Sylkow indicates to one of his regimental commanders the direction in which he wants his troops to go. (IWM HU5613) Right: A dead crewman lies sprawled half in, half out of the turret hatch of his knocked-out PzKpfw III. The tank has been hit in the side by 2pdr armour-piercing shells at least three times. (IWM STT3217)

but neither were they a spent force, as the British were to find out.

While the Guards Brigade had been extending their defensive line the 11th Infantry Brigade, some ten miles to their rear, had tried once again to prise Kampfgruppe Bach from its defensive position in Halfaya Pass. However, the Germans fully realised that they had nowhere to retreat and fought with a desperation that only this sort of situation can create. Badly outnumbered (although not out-gunned—Bach's force had yet to lose any of its 88s), the defenders held on. Messervy, realising that infantry alone could not take the position, disregarded Beresford-Peirse's order to move the 4th RTR immediately to join the cruiser tanks of the 7th Armoured Brigade. The Matildas would be reassigned only when significant inroads into the Axis defences had been made. This was not to happen on 16 June.

On the British left flank the 5th Light Division spent the day trying to work its way round the southern flank of the 2nd and 6th RTR. To prevent this the now heavily outnumbered British staged a step-by-step withdrawal back to the frontier. They tried and failed on several occasions

to bring the German armour to battle, but the panzers would quickly withdraw behind a hastily assembled screen of infantry and anti-tank guns, against which the cruiser tanks were powerless.

If the British tanks stood their ground PzKpfw IVs (armed with a 75mm gun) would come forward and shell the few 25pdr field guns still with the tattered 7th Armoured Brigade. This would inevitably cause them to pull back. The PzKpfw IIIs and IVs could then sit outside the 500yds effective range of the British 2pdr tank guns and pick off the lightly armoured cruisers at a leisurely rate. If the British moved forward the panzers retired behind an anti-tank gun screen, and all the while motorised infantry, armoured cars and light tanks would be working their way round the brigade's flank. Sitting it out, it soon became apparent, was not an option.

The other major problem the British faced was that of mechanical reliability. The A9, A10 and A13 cruiser tanks of the 2nd RTR had always been poor in this respect and now, during the retreat to the frontier, it was discovered that the Crusaders of the 6th RTR were just as bad. Not

Left: A DAK despatch rider, his message clamped between his teeth, leaves an SdKfz 251 command half-track to carry new instructions to a unit in the field. (IWM PC249)

only were the British losing the tank-versus-panzer battle, but they were also losing their fight against the harsh desert conditions.

By the morning of 16 June the 7th Armoured Brigade had only 48 operational tanks left. With this meagre force the British tried to slow down the penetration of their front line, principally to allow the 7th Armoured Division Support Group to fall back on their flank before they became cut off. This they successfully managed to do, fighting running battles with the advancing German motorised and mechanised force throughout the day. Rommel had been present at several of these brief but bloody engagements and had quickly come to the conclusion that if he could apply just a little more pressure he would be able to smash through to Halfaya Pass, relieve Bach's beleaguered defenders and trap a sizeable number of British troops.

At 4 p.m. he ordered the 15th Panzer Division to disengage permanently all its remaining motorised and mechanised forces from in front of Fort Capuzzo, leaving behind only

a small covering force, to be supplemented by Italian infantry now moving up from the Tobruk area. Neumann-Sylkow's formation was ordered to move with all possible speed to link up with the inner flank of the 5th Light Division near Sidi Omar, giving Rommel the additional punch he needed to smash through the British defences. This switch of thrust was not appreciated by the British until 6 a.m. on 17 June, when the combined force of the 5th Light and 15th Panzer Divisions fell upon the weak screen of British troops west of Sidi Suleiman.

The 7th Armoured Brigade was by now incapable of holding its own ground: in the morning of 17 June only nine cruiser tanks were left in fully functioning order. Luckily for them, the 7th Armoured Division Support Group (Brigadier Jock Campbell) had fallen back through the formation during the night and the 25pdrs of the 3rd and 4th Regi-

Right: The commander of a DAK PzKpfw III scans the horizon for enemy tanks. (IWM HU32660)

ments Royal Horse Artillery, along with the 1st Battalion King's Royal Rifle Corps and 2nd Battalion Rifle Brigade, were able to shoulder the burden of the defence against the panzer thrust.

Luckily for Beresford-Peirse, Major-General Frank Messervy, in command of the Guards at Capuzzo and the 11th Infantry Brigade at Halfaya, had late on the 16th realised the danger his force was in and had ordered the remaining Matildas of the 4th and 7th RTR to disengage and make their way to the top of the Halfaya escarpment. There they joined the 2nd Battalion Cameron Highlanders, at that point deadlocked in front of Bach's defensive positions.

Leaving a small rearguard to pin them in position, the infantry and tanks fanned out to form a narrow corridor from Fort Capuzzo along the southern lip of the Halfaya escarpment. The 7th Armoured Division

Support Group fell back on this position and, with the remaining mobile tanks of the 7th Armoured Brigade, along with an attachment of motorised infantry, formed a flank guard, covering the route from the escarpment to Buq Buq. Rommel, still hoping to catch the majority of the British force in a pocket between Halfaya and Bardia, ordered the 5th Light and 15th Panzer Divisions to push hard to the north. If the panzers could break through quickly the victory would be decisive: there would then be few organised Allied units left between DAK and Alexandria.

However, Neumann-Sylkow and Ravenstein were unable to smash through as instructed. The German panzers crashed headlong into a well-prepared defence of hull-down Matildas, dug-in 25pdrs and dogged British infantry. For the 15th Panzer Division it was a virtual re-run of the futile assault against Fort Capuzzo. For the 5th Light Division it was the first time during the battle they had encountered a determined defence. Without their 88mm guns, still some way to the rear, the PzKpfw IIIs and IVs were unable to make a dent in the British position. And all the while the battle raged the motorised infantry of the 22nd Guards Brigade raced eastwards to safety. The British held on until 4 p.m., when the last troops fell back through the corridor. The Matildas and motorised artillery and infantry of the rearguard pulled back unmolested, the German troops too exhausted by two days of constant fighting and manoeuvre to follow up.

A little later the tired panzer crews linked up with the dishevelled defenders of Halfaya Pass. Rommel was full of praise for Bach, whose small detachment had held out so valiantly, but he was less happy with Neumann-Sylkow and Ravenstein, who he felt had not acted quickly enough in securing a breakthrough to create

the pocket he so desperately wanted. The British escape was, however, not really their fault. Both Creagh and, more significantly, Messervy had realised the potential danger early and had taken steps to make sure that Rommel did not get the decisive victory he wanted. The same could not be said of Beresford-Peirse, and to a lesser extent Wavell, both of whom had continued to press for tank attacks long after they had ceased to be feasible (to be fair, this was in part because of the terrible communications existing between the front and the rear HQs.)

The men in the field fully realised that the way to stop Rommel was not to attempt to bring about a clash of armour—the Germans held a decisive advantage in quality of equipment and doctrine—but somehow to bring to bear the Allied advantage in infantry (at this point in time quality, although later this became an

advantage in quantity as well). This sea change in perceptions—to bring about victory not by dramatic armoured manoeuvre but by dogged attrition—would not be taken up by British High Command until a year later, with the arrival of Montgomery in North Africa.

Operation 'Battleaxe' was a failure for the British: they had neither captured the Halfaya Heights nor relieved the besieged Tobruk garrison. However, Rommel, who had taken the opportunity with which he was presented to turn the British offensive into a German counter-offensive, had also failed to achieve his goals. His counter-attack had forced the British back to their start line but no

Below: A slightly wounded Royal Tank Regiment crewman receives medical attention from one of his companions on his Matilda tank. (IWM E13099)

significant numbers of enemy troops had been captured, and the damage caused to DAK during the last day's fighting and the abortive assault on Fort Capuzzo ruled out any major offensive in the near future. Both sides' attacking capability had been blunted.

Rommel lost 1,277 men during 'Battleaxe' (just under half of them Italian troops) whilst the Allies had taken 969 casualties. The British had also lost 91 tanks, many of them easily repairable but abandoned in the retreat. The Germans, who had control of the battlefield after the action, were able eventually to recover and repair all but 12 of their panzer losses. They even repaired a few Matildas and added them to their inventory.

The failure of Operation 'Battleaxe' led directly to the dismissal of both Beresford-Peirse and Wavell from their commands. Wavell was

replaced by General Sir Claude Auchinleck, previously commander-in-chief in India, whilst Beresford-Peirse gave way to Lieutenant-General Sir Alan Cunningham, fresh from his victories in East Africa, where he had soundly beaten the Italians.

Auchinleck was Churchill's choice. Tall, ruggedly handsome and aggressive in tone, he seemed just the person to raise the spirits of the dejected men of the Western Desert Force. However, Churchill was to be bitterly disappointed. Optimistic and aggressive Auchinleck may have been, but he was not going to be bullied into a premature offensive by the Prime Minister. Churchill, who applied immediate pressure for the early re-

Above: Two Italians who obviously could not read English! On their way to the rear these two soldiers decided to stop for a rest and an amused AFPU (Army Film and Photographic Unit) cameraman could not resist taking their picture. The two bewildered Italians look on, 21 October 1941. (IWM E6127)

sumption of the offensive, became quickly disenchanted with his new commander. Auchinleck was firm in his belief that 'no further offensive in the Western Desert should be contemplated until base is secure'. He was sure that, at least in part, Wavell's failure was due to his having to juggle too many campaigns at once. A new offensive in North Africa could not begin until the Syrian affair (the campaign against Vichy France in the Middle East) was brought to a successful conclusion. There was also the problem of re-equipping the battered 7th Armoured Division: replacement tanks and new drafts of men were desperately needed. Churchill was dismayed: he wanted an almost immediate counter-attack. Auchinleck was unmoved. The offensive would not resume until the end of the summer at least, and autumn was much more likely.

As well as an intrusive Prime Minister, Auchinleck also faced a major problem in that he knew very little about the men he was to command. A regular Indian Army officer, he had

Below: General Sir Archibald Wavell (right) appraises his replacement, General Sir Claude Auchinleck, of the strategic situation prior to his departure for India, 8 September 1941. (IWM E5448)

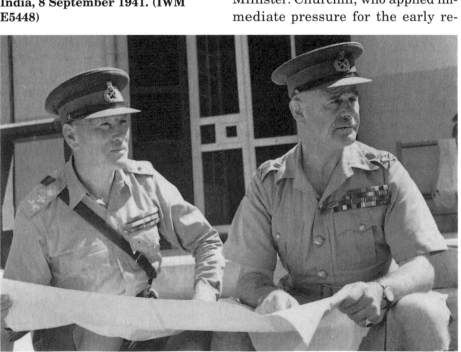

Left: A Junkers Ju 87B Stuka over the North African coast. (IWM HU2924)

command the Italian Expeditionary Force in Russia—and was replaced by General Ettore Bastico, a personal friend of Mussolini, eager to increase his influence on the back of Rommel's achievements. Bastico was pompous, highly autocratic and an unusually ineffective commander, unpopular with virtually all of his senior officers—paradoxically, just the sort of man Rommel wanted. At the same time the Italian Chief of Staff, General Ugo Cavallero, who disliked Bastico intensely, proposed and pushed through a plan to create an Axis army group command, under Rommel's direct control. Bastico, a general far senior in rank to Rommel, would no doubt have been greatly angered when he found out he held little more than a figurehead appointment. Rommel was also promoted to *General der Panzertruppen*, a rank more befitting an army group commander. By the end of August his new command, to be known as Panzergruppe Afrika, was taking shape.

DAK now consisted of the 15th Panzer Division (Neumann-Sylkow), the 21st Panzer Division (von Ravenstein) and the curiously titled Division Zbv. Afrika, known commonly as the Afrika Division (soon to become the 90th Light Division) commanded by Lieutenant-General Max Summerman. This last formation, although German, contained the 2nd Italian Motorised Artillery Regiment. It also had as part of its complement the 361st 'Afrika' Infantry Regiment, two battalions of battle-hardened ex-French Foreign Legionnaires who were veterans of years of desert campaigning. In addition DAK also had attached the Italian Savona Infantry Division. The whole corps was commanded by General Ludwig Crue-

served all his career (except for a single ten-month period) in India or the Middle East. He knew Frank Messervy, commander of the 4th Indian Division, well, but had to rely on second-hand reports to assess the ability of those he was asked to appoint to his staff and divisional or brigade command. The man he chose to lead the new 8th Army (as the Western Desert Force was officially renamed in September) would also face problems with his new command.

Cunningham was a gunner by training and the forces he had led to victory in Ethiopia had been infan-

Below: A group of Italian officers chats to the crew of a Breda 20mm anti-aircraft gun. (IWM HU32768)

try divisions. However, Auchinleck was still of the belief that the action of armour would be decisive in the Western Desert, a view reinforced in talks he had with Wavell before his departure. So Cunningham, who had no experience of highly mobile manoeuvre warfare, was perhaps a strange choice. Maybe Auchinleck listened too readily to those who enthused over his leadership qualities—and then again perhaps he appointed Cunningham just to annoy Churchill, who wanted Maitland Wilson to take over as Beresford-Peirse's successor.

The end of 'Battleaxe' also saw changes in the Axis command structure. On 12 July General Gariboldi returned to Italy—he was later to

Right: A 2in mortar crew and Bren gun team from a Sikh regiment take cover behind a rocky outcrop, 6 August 1941. (IWM E4667)

well. The other formation that made up Rommel's Panzergruppe Afrika, the Italian XXI Corps (General Enea Navarini), consisted of four infantry divisions (Pavia, Bologna, Brescia and Trento).

As to sop to General Bastico, he was given nominal control of the remaining Italian formation in Cyrenaica, the Corpo d'Armata di Manovra (CAM), commanded by General Gastone Gambara. In reality, however, Gambara took his battle orders from Rommel, and Bastico, although technically Rommel's superior, had little effect on strategic or tactical planning. CAM consisted of the Ariete Armoured Division and the Trieste Motorised Division. In addition the formation also contained the RECAM (Raggruppamento Esplorante) reconnaissance group of two tank battalions, one motorised artillery regiment and three battalions of motorised infantry (two of them Blackshirt formations).

Rommel tested his new command as soon as he could, launching Operation 'Midsummer Night's Dream' on 14 September. A reconnaissance in force by elements of the 21st Panzer Division, the mission had as its ostensible objective the capture and destruction of a large British supply dump situated (so DAK intelligence thought) some 20 miles south-east of Sidi Omar. The raid would also test the ability of the 11th Hussars and 4th South African Armoured Car Regiment, whose vehicles patrolled the deep desert in this area. Rommel wanted to find out just how these frontier forces would react. He suspected that the British were building up substantial supplies in the area in preparation for a major offensive: his intelligence sources had informed him that men and equipment had of late been flooding into Egypt at an ever-increasing rate. If he ran into stiff opposition his suspicions would be confirmed.

However, this did not happen and the three small Kampfgruppen assigned to penetrate the British line did so with relative ease. By midday the supposed supply dump had been reached. Unfortunately the position turned out to have been long abandoned, and all that could be found were several crates and a pile of empty beer bottles. Nevertheless, this and the lack of opposition were enough to confirm to Rommel that the British did not, after all, plan a major offensive. But, to be sure, he ordered that the units should push on to Sofafi, another 25 miles to the east.

As the DAK formations neared the town they came under both aerial and artillery bombardment and ground resistance stiffened. Unfortunately at this point two of the three

Left: Staff of the 21st Panzer Division Headquarters plan their next move. (IWM HU5596)

German columns came to a halt owing to a lack of fuel. The bombardment continued and German casualties began to mount (they included Rommel's driver). The decision was made to withdraw as soon as refuelling had been completed. The apparent correctness of the order was reinforced when a truck from the headquarters of the 4th South African Armoured Car Regiment was captured, full of papers. These seemed to indicate that, far from attacking, the Allies were preparing to pull back to better positions further to the east. Rommel was satisfied: the British in Egypt presented no threat in the foreseeable future. Unfortunately Rommel was wrong.

The ever-cautious Allies were in fact building up for an offensive. If Rommel's columns had pushed on past Sofafi they would have discovered the dumps that DAK was so worried about. The documents captured from the South Africans were in fact orders for a redeployment of frontier forces—the unit was due to be pulled back for rest and recuperation, their place taken by another formation. There was no planned general withdrawal. The British supply dumps had been positioned over 50 miles to the rear (far too far away to be of practical use in Rommel's view) precisely because a hit-and-run raid was feared.

By the end of September the 8th Army, the new formation to undertake Auchinleck's planned offensive, was almost complete. It consisted of two corps. XIII Corps, commanded by Lieutenant-General Alfred Godwin-Austen (another command choice made with Churchill's disapproval) was made up of the 4th Indian Divi-

sion (Messervy), the New Zealand Division (Major-General Bernard Freyberg) and the 1st Army Tank Brigade (Brigadier H. R. B. Watkins); XXX Corps was made up of the 7th Armoured Division (now commanded by Major General 'Strafer' Gott), the 1st South African Division, (Major-General G. E. Brink) and the 22nd Guards Brigade. Also attached was Major-General Alec Gatehouse's 4th Armoured Brigade Group. The Tob-

ruk garrison had also changed in composition. The 9th Australian Division, which had hitherto formed the core of the defence, was gradually pulled out by sea and sent to join the 7th Australian Division in Syria. It

Below: Polish infantry disembark at Tobruk as part of the relief force allowing the Australian 9th Division to withdraw, September 1941. (IWM E5053)

was replaced by the British 70th Division, the Polish 1st Carpathian Brigade and a Czech battalion. In addition, more Matilda infantry tanks were supplied to the garrison and the tank forces in Tobruk were reorganised into the 32nd Army Tank Brigade. Auchinleck did not want to pull out the Australians, probably the best infantry he had in the Western Desert, but pressure from the Australian government to enforce the agreement that the Australian divisions should serve together forced Churchill to order their redeployment. It is a measure of the effectiveness of this transfer of troops (although three Royal Navy ships were lost during the operation) that Rommel fully expected his next major assault on Tobruk, planned for the 20 November, to be met by Australian rather than British or Polish infantry.

The late summer and early autumn of 1941 had seen almost continuous fighting along the Tobruk perimeter, although Rommel had been careful not to commit too many of his precious German formations. The garrison was constantly shelled and dive-bombed by German and Italian aircraft, and there were regular infantry clashes as Axis and Allied patrols jostled for more favourable positions along the outer edge of the siege line. However, until Rommel had built up a sufficient number of troops, supplies and siege equipment to break down the garrison in an assault, his main way of trying to force it into surrender was to attempt to cut off its supplies. Nevertheless, despite the best efforts of the *Luftwaffe* and *Regia Aeronautica* to halt the flow into and out of the port, enough men and material were brought in to make the defence a sustainable, even if a very uncomfortable, one.

To help Rommel in his planned assault on Tobruk Hitler had him assigned a special siege train. Known

Above and below: A dawn patrol works its way through the Tobruk perimeter wire as it sets out to reconnoitre enemy positions, 12 **September 1941. Some hours later the infantry return, having taken a single casualty whilst in enemy territory. (IWM E5499/E5501)**

as Artillery Group 104, it consisted of five units containing some very heavy guns—nine 210mm howitzers, twelve French 105mm guns, 46 French 150mm guns, 36 Italian 105mm guns, 84 Italian 149mm guns and twelve 120mm naval guns, all of them under the command of Major-General Karl Boettcher. This arsenal was positioned to the south-east of the Tobruk perimeter, and once its considerable ammunition supply difficulties had been sorted out it began to pour a murderous fire on to the defenders.

Rommel, confident that the Allies were not going to attempt another relief of Tobruk, was in no rush to begin his attack. His previous information, obtained from Operation 'Midsummer Night's Dream', was supported by his German agents in Egypt. These sources told him that the reinforcements landing in Egypt were on the whole moving east, not west. It was their opinion that they were moving to Syria to protect Britain's oil supplies, should the Caucasus fall to the *Wehrmacht*. Little did Rommel know that his organisation had been thoroughly penetrated by British intelligence and some of the agents turned.

The opening of the Allied offensive on 18 November came as a complete surprise. It is interesting to note that Rommel's Chief of Intelligence, Major F. W. von Mellenthin, in his mem-

oirs, argues that Rommel's categorical denials of the possibility of an Allied offensive were made to bolster Italian morale, even though he knew an attack was imminent. The only evidence to support this is that Rommel did order the 21st Panzer Division to a position south of Gambut, between Tobruk and the frontier. This move would have in

any case been prudent, to prevent British interference whilst he carried out his assault on the port. If he really did suspect an offensive surely he would have cancelled, or at the very least postponed, his planned attack on Tobruk and have ordered a much more defensive posture and aggressive patrolling to ascertain Allied intentions.

Right: The German crew of an Italian 149mm heavy gun prepares to fire another round during the bombardment of Allied positions, November/December 1941. Artillery Group 104 acquired several Italian heavy artillery pieces to enhance its siege-breaking capabilities. (IWM HU31552)

CHAPTER FOUR

OPERATION 'CRUSADER'

During the summer and autumn of 1941 all Rommel's plans for the North African campaign were affected by his poor level of supply, of men, of material and especially of fuel. Rommel, the Italian High Command and OKH (the German Army High Command, headed by Halder) were all of the opinion that future success in the Western Desert depended upon the capture of Tobruk. Rommel confirmed to his superiors in July that the capture of the port, which would

give him a high-capacity, deep-water facility, close to the front line, was his next priority. He hoped to be able to launch a full-scale attack on the town in September, but continual shipping losses in the Mediterranean forced postponement after postponement, until the date was finally fixed for 20 November. DAK was actually in position to strike a week earlier, but the assault was put back to await a favourable full moon. If Rommel had struck earlier, the entire course of the desert war might have been

different, because on 18 November Auchinleck launched Operation 'Crusader', the long-awaited Allied offensive which would result in Rommel's first serious reversal of fortune.

As has been stated earlier, Rommel had convinced himself and the majority of his German colleagues that no Allied attack was in the offing. Bastico, however, kept informed by

Below: An 88mm anti-aircraft gun in action with Italian troops. (IWM MH5859)

Right: CV33/35 tankettes on the move. This outdated and obsolete Italian vehicle soldiered on throughout the desert campaign, despite having paper thin armour and only machine guns for armament. Remarkably, it gained a limited new lease of life in 1942 when several were refitted as flame-thrower tanks. (IWM HU28383)

Italian military intelligence, felt that an assault was imminent. On 29 October General Gambara, in command of CAM, the only Italian formation not controlled directly by Rommel, requested that his forces be placed at Bir El Gubi and Bir Hacheim, just in case the British tried an outflanking manoeuvre through the desert. To this Rommel gladly acceded: the Ariete and Trieste divisions were not needed for the assault on Tobruk and their positioning on his southern flank would relieve DAK units of the necessity of garrisoning the area. It was lucky for Rommel that the well-commanded and equipped (by Italian standards) Ariete Armoured Division was positioned forward at Bir El Gubi because it was here that the first major clash of Operation 'Crusader' was to take place—a clash that was to result in a significant Italian victory.

On the eve of 'Crusader' the Ariete Division could muster 137 M13/40 tanks and 52 CV33/35 tankettes, split between the 132nd Medium and 32nd Light Armoured Regiments. Infantry support was provided by the 8th (Motorised) Bersaglieri Regiment, and four battalions of artillery (three 75mm, one 105mm) gave the formation its long-range fire support. Anti-

tank gun cover for the division was provided by three batteries of truck-mounted 102mm naval guns, which were to prove to be extremely effective in the battles to come.

As well as the Ariete covering the southern approaches to Cyrenaica, Rommel had deployed the Italian Savona Division (General Fedele de Giorgis) between Sollum and Sidi Omar, strengthening them with two German infantry battalions, a motor-

ised infantry battalion (in reserve) and twelve 88mm anti-tank/anti-aircraft guns. The entire 25-mile front was covered by a large belt of mines, and at several points along the line (Sollum, Halfaya Pass, Halfway House, Fort Capuzzo and Sidi Omar) there were extensive field fortifications.

The expanse of desert between Sidi Omar, Gabr Saleh and Bir El Gubi (a roughly 60-mile east-to-west gap

Below: A Vickers machine-gun team of the 2nd Battalion King's Own Royal Regiment fires on an enemy position during the siege of Tobruk, 10 November 1941. (IWM E6442)

53

along the Trigh El Abd, the track from Bir El Gubi to the Egyptian frontier) was patrolled by the 3rd and 33rd Reconnaissance Battalions from the 15th and 21st Panzer Divisions. Further to the south, around oases in the deep desert, several Italian Arditi and German Oasis companies were based, just in case the Allies were foolish enough to mount a major attack from this direction.

The majority of the Axis formations were deployed around Tobruk, ready for Rommel's planned assault. The Brescia Division held the western approaches to the port, the Trento Division the southern perimeter and the Bologna Division the eastern sector of the siege lines. The 15th and 21st Panzer Divisions, along with the Afrika Division, were allotted the task of breaking into the Tobruk defences. The two armoured divisions had between them a total of approximately 240 battle tanks—70 PzKpfw IIs, 130 PzKpfw IIIs, 35 PzKpfw IVs and half a dozen or so captured Matilda infantry tanks. The three German formations also had available 23 88mm guns and 136 other anti-tank (mostly 50mm) guns. They were deployed to the south-east of the port, west of Gambut, now home to Panzergruppe Afrika Headquarters.

Above: Two A9 cruiser tanks of the 3rd Armoured Brigade move to a trouble spot on the Tobruk perimeter, 12 September 1941. (IWM E5547)

The Italian Pavia Division was held in reserve to the north of Sidi Rezegh.

Lieutenant-General Sir Alan Cunningham was assigned two Allied corps for his offensive. The spearhead of the attack would be provided by XXX Corps (Lieutenant-General Willoughby M. Norrie), consisting of a revamped 7th Armoured Division, the 1st South African Division and the 22nd Guards Brigade. Flank

54

cover and support for the main thrust would be given by XIII Corps (Lieutenant-General Alfred Godwin-Austin), made up of the 4th Indian Division and the 2nd New Zealand Division, tank support being provided by the 1st Army Tank Brigade. The British fielded many more tanks for Operation 'Crusader' than did the Axis. The 7th Armoured Division alone contained 491 battle tanks, more than twice the combined total of the 15th and 21st Panzer Divisions!

The three brigades that made up the 7th Armoured Division were organised as follows. The 7th Armoured Brigade (7th Hussars, 2nd and 6th RTR) had a total of 168 tanks, 71 Crusaders, 71 A13s and 26 A10s; the 22nd Armoured Brigade (3rd and 4th County of London Yeomanry and 2nd Royal Gloucestershire Hussars) contained 158 Crusaders; and the 4th Armoured Brigade (8th Hussars, 3rd and 5th RTR) had 165 Stuart light tanks. The 1st Army Tank Brigade supporting XIII Corps consisted of 132 tanks, two-thirds of them Matildas (42nd and 44th RTR) and the rest Valentines (8th RTR). The 32nd Army Tank Brigade in Tobruk was made up of the 1st RTR, with 32 old cruiser and 25 Mk VI light tanks, and the 4th RTR, plus D Squadron 7th RTR, with some 70 Matildas.

The plan was for the 7th Armoured Division to push across the frontier south of Sidi Omar to Gabr Saleh, where it would halt. This mass of armour would inevitably attract the attention of Rommel's panzers. The 15th and 21st Panzer Divisions would attack on ground of Cunningham's choosing and be defeated. Meanwhile, on the left, the 1st South African Division would shore up the flank of the advance, while XIII Corps invested and defeated the Axis forces on the frontier. After the defeat of the German armoured formations (note that the Italian Ariete Armoured Division was not considered a threat)

and the collapse of the frontier defences, an advance would be made on Tobruk; this would be supported by a sortie from the besieged town by elements of the 70th Infantry Division and 32nd Army Tank Brigade (Operation 'Pop').

This rather simplistic and naive plan was, however, founded upon three fundamental misconceptions. The first was that only the defeat of German formations mattered. The Italians, it was thought, would provide no stiff opposition to the advance, either from the cross-border attack or the Tobruk break-out that was to follow. Operation 'Crusader' was to teach the Allies not to underestimate Italian fighting ability.

The second misconception was that German armoured warfare theory was the same as British tank doctrine. The British saw the role of the armoured division as one of bringing to battle and defeating the enemy's tank formations. The British High Command envisaged armoured warfare as being akin to naval warfare, where fleets of armour sought to bring to battle, outmanoeuvre and defeat the enemy's fleet. Many British tank commanders, especially those from traditional cavalry regiments, saw the tank as a modern-day steed. Victory would be won by dash-

ing charges against the German panzer formations. Then infantry units would be safe to carry out their task of defeating enemy infantry and consolidating the ground gained. German Blitzkrieg theory stressed the avoidance of tank-versus-tank battles. Panzers were to seek out weak points in the enemy defences (and these were most likely to be infantry, rather than armoured, formations) and bring about victory as much by psychological defeat as by physical destruction. Rommel, therefore, had no urge at all to confront the 7th Armoured Division *en masse*, both because it contained the majority of the British armour and because it was definitely not a weak spot in the Allied order of battle.

Finally, Cunningham assumed that Rommel would have to take action if a corps of Allied troops crossed the border and ensconced itself firmly in territory previously held by the Axis. However, the loss of a few hundred square miles of desert meant nothing to Rommel as long as the loss did not endanger his strategic position or deflect him from his main objective, the capture of Tobruk.

Below: A German LFH 18 105mm field gun firing over open sights at a ground target. (IWM RML639)

Left: German prisoners bring in one of their wounded comrades in a blanket, 18 November 1941. (IWM E6792)

Rommel firmly believed at the outset that Operation 'Crusader' was a feint, intended to draw troops away from Tobruk and undermine his planned assault. Not until Gott, fed up with a lack of response from the Axis forces, pushed on north of his original Gabr Saleh stop line did he realise the true nature of the Allied offensive. Then, and only then, with communications to the frontier and Tobruk directly threatened, did he react. Of course, this meant that in all the subsequent operations the Allies were now working outside the parameters of their original plan, and were reacting to events just as much as the Axis were. Unfortunately for the British High Command, the Germans were much more adept at improvising than they were.

Rommel should have got an inkling of British intentions when, in the evening of 17 November, German intelligence reported that the Allies had lapsed into total radio silence, something they had previously done before both 'Brevity' and 'Battleaxe'. However, he was not to be deflected from his plans to assault Tobruk. When on the 18th Cruewell and Ravenstein, alarmed at reports from the 3rd and 33rd Reconnaissance Battalions of large numbers of Allied armoured cars pushing across the Trigh el Abd, advised Rommel to move an armoured Kampfgruppe to Gabr Saleh, he told them, 'We must not lose our nerves.'

By the morning of the 19th he could no longer deny that something was afoot, but he still hoped it was just a diversion. Nevertheless, with reports of enemy tank forces to the north of the Trigh el Abd, he was forced to take action. The 21st Panzer Division was ordered to move south towards Gabr Saleh, whilst the 15th Panzer Division was to concentrate at an assembly area south of Gambut. The decision to commit the 21st Panzer Division to battle, without waiting for support, was much more risky than Rommel appreciated. If the advance had been a reconnaissance in force the panzers could probably have seen off the enemy, but the whole of the 7th Armoured Division had been ordered to congregate at

Right: Royal Tank Regiment Matildas on the move, 18 November 1941. (IWM E6600)

Gabr Saleh. If they were there when the 21st Panzer Division arrived, there was not much hope of an Axis victory. Fortunately for Rommel, Gott had earlier dispersed his armour. The 7th Armoured Division, on the move since the morning of the 18th, had not met the armoured counter-attack it was expecting. Instead, the German reconnaissance screen had been brushed aside and the advance had been carried through, largely without opposition.

In the morning of the 19th Gott was faced with a dilemma. Either he continued to sit where he was at Gabr Saleh and risk being ignored, or he pushed the 7th Armoured Division on and abandoned the plan laid down by Cunningham. Deciding to take advantage of the enemy's lethargic reaction, he resolved to drive on towards Tobruk. However, he could not do this without splitting his force.

Gott wanted to seize Sidi Rezegh, less than 20 miles from the southern perimeter of besieged Tobruk. With its double ridge line and airfield, the position, if captured in its entirety, would provide a good defensive location and a well-positioned springboard for a drive on Tobruk. However, if Sidi Rezegh were to be taken, Bir el Gubi would also have to be attacked. Any enemy force left there unmolested would be able to strike into the line of communication of the 7th Armoured Division, making its position further forward untenable in the long term. Gott therefore despatched the 22nd Armoured Brigade to Bir el Gubi with orders to defeat, or at least hold in check, any enemy force based there.

The right flank of the 7th Armoured Division also presented a problem. Any push towards Sidi Rezegh would create a yawning gap between the formation and the 2nd

Above: A Stuart light tank of the Royal Irish Hussars moves at speed across the desert, 28 October 1941. (IWM E6293)

New Zealand Division, still on the frontier. Therefore Gott decided to leave the 4th Armoured Brigade at Gabr Saleh, to act as a link between the two formations. This left only the 7th Armoured Brigade and the Divisional Support Group to press on. However, Gott was confident that if he moved fast enough he could capture Sidi Rezegh before the Germans could react effectively. Sidi Rezegh would not have to be held for very long, the 70th Division would quickly break out of the Tobruk perimeter to link up with them and the 2nd New Zealand Division and the 1st South African Division were not too far behind.

Thus, in the early afternoon of 19 November, when the 5th Panzer

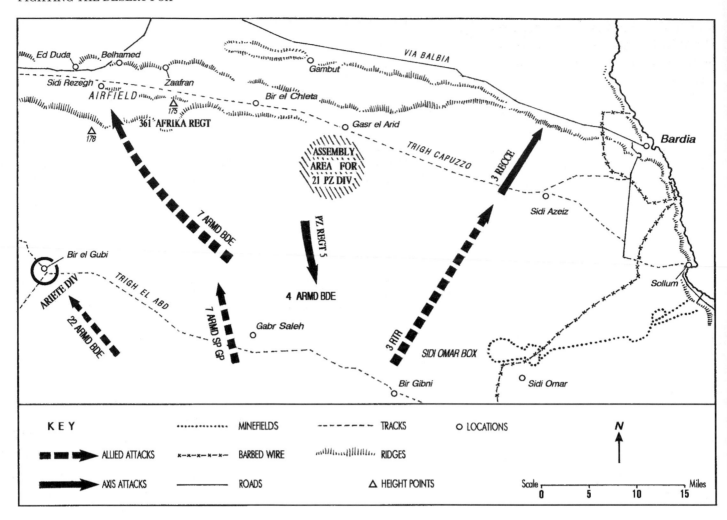

Above: Operation 'Crusader': the armoured clash, 19 November 1941.

Regiment, supported by twelve 105mm guns and four 88s, made contact with the British just north of Gabr Saleh, it only had to contend with the Stuart light tanks of the 4th Armoured Brigade. To make matters even worse for the British, the panzers attacked shortly after the 3rd RTR had been detached from the Brigade to pursue the 3rd Reconnaissance Battalion back across the Trigh Capuzzo towards Bardia, the armoured cars of the King's Dragoon Guards having failed to do so.

In the running battle that followed the British had 23 tanks knocked out while the Germans lost only seven vehicles. The 4th Armoured Brigade, pushed back over the Trigh El Abd, left the battlefield to the Germans

and they were able to recover and repair all but three of their losses. The British, who were able to return later in the operation, managed to recover twelve of theirs. The engagement was notable for something other than the first time the Stuart tank saw action. After the battle Brigadier Gatehouse, Commander of the 4th Armoured Brigade, in his message to Cunningham claimed as definite 19 German tanks destroyed. This over-estimating of British tank success was the first of many during Operation 'Crusader', and helped to build a false picture at 8th Army Headquarters, who rapidly came to believe that DAK was being destroyed on the field of battle.

The 22nd Armoured Brigade fared no better in its clash with the Ariete Division at Bir el Gubi. The Italians were well dug in, their main defen-

sive position consisting of three large emplacements linked by trenches, fronted by barbed wire and a smattering of anti-tank mines. The mass of Axis armour was drawn up on the left of the Italian line. The 22nd Armoured Brigade, made up of three Yeomanry regiments, none of whom had previous combat experience, decided to assault the fortifications. Deploying into one long line, they charged the Axis positions like the cavalry of old. The result was a disaster.

The Italians, somewhat stunned by this wild dash for glory, failed to react quickly, and as a result the emplacement at the right-hand end of the defence line was quickly overrun. However, the charge was brought to an abrupt halt before the other two strongpoints and in front of the Italian armour. Dug-in 47-32 anti-tank guns, the 47mm guns on the M13/40 tanks and especially the seven 102mm portee naval guns in the front line caused heavy casualties amongst the Crusaders.

The success on the left flank of the British attack was short-lived. The Italian infantry and gun crews who had initially stood up, hands in the air, and waited to be taken prisoner found that no Allied infantry were accompanying the assault. With no one to surrender to, they quickly decided to return to their guns and the Crusaders were once more under fire, this time from very close range in flank and rear.

The attack, which began at midday, petered out at around 5 p.m., with the tanks of the 22nd Armoured Brigade withdrawing eastwards into leaguer, leaving the battlefield to the Italians and enabling them to claim a victory. The Italians had 34 tanks knocked out, and eight 47mm anti-tank guns and one 65mm infantry gun were lost in the action. Many of the Axis vehicles were later recovered and repaired. The British lost 50 Crusaders, the majority of them being permanently disabled by the Italians. Again the British overestimated the damage done to the enemy, claiming that they had knocked out as much Axis armour as they had lost. The situation was further misrepresented by the brigade's claim that German troops and 88mm guns were present at Bir el Gubi; in fact, they were not.

The only real Allied success of 19 November came when, late in the afternoon, cruiser tanks of the 2nd and 6th RTR, along with armoured cars of the 4th South African Armoured Car Regiment, overran Sidi Rezegh airfield, capturing several Italian air-

Right, top and centre: Italian M13/40 tanks on the move across the desert. (IWM HU28363/HU28364) Right, bottom: Italian Bersaglieri infantry in action. (IWM HU28384)

craft on the ground and destroying several more trying to take off and make their escape.

Fortunately for Cunningham and Gott, Rommel and Cruewell failed to appreciate the true nature of the Allied offensive. Panzergruppe Afrika Headquarters, after collating the day's reports, felt that three major Allied forces were operating against them. The first had seized Sidi Rezegh airfield, the second was operating between Gabr Saleh and Bir el Gubi and the third was pushing north across the Trigh Capuzzo towards the Via Balbia, where it could then either swing east to Bardia or move west to Tobruk.

Below: An Australian 2pdr anti-tank gun mounted on the back of a truck (portee) engages Italian armour, November 1941. According to the photographer, this gun was attacked by three tanks: one was knocked out, one was damaged and forced to retire and one fled the scene. (IWM E3734E)

Rommel was also aware of a fourth force, moving across the deep desert towards Jarabub and Jalo, some 120 miles to the south of the Cyrenaica bulge. This advance threatened to outflank the entire Axis defence line, but Rommel made a conscious decision to ignore it. This was partially because he just did not have any troops left in reserve to counter the threat, but also because he calculated that so far into the Sahara the Allies would only be able to keep a limited number of forces in the field. In this he was right. The Allied formation, called E-Force for Operation 'Crusader', consisted of the 29th Indian Infantry Brigade (Motorised) and the 6th and 7th South African Armoured Car Regiments. It was intended to force Rommel to pull much of his force back to cover his southern flank but instead it just diluted the forces available for the main Allied thrust.

The Allied force at Sidi Rezegh could be held in check by the Afrika Division and the Pavia Division, both

of whom were fortuitously in the area, the German formation preparing to lead the assault on Tobruk and the Italian division in reserve, just in case the garrison attempted a break out. To bolster their position further, Artillery Group 104 was deployed to the north of the airfield, within range of both Tobruk and Sidi Rezegh.

The advance of the second force to the west had been stopped by the Ariete Division at Bir el Gubi and the 5th Panzer Regiment had blunted any northward move the force might have been contemplating. Without enough motorised and mechanised forces to engage all the mobile Allied formations in the desert, Rommel felt that this was the force he could leave alone for the time being. Being the furthest away, and with its nose severely bloodied, it was unlikely to make a concerted drive on Tobruk.

The third enemy force, the one that had chased the 3rd Reconnaissance Battalion back across the Trigh Capuzzo, was a different matter entirely. It threatened to attack Tobruk directly down the Via Balbia (if it did so it would surely overrun Panzergruppe Headquarters at Gambut), or it might assault Bardia and the frontier defences from the west, their only unfortified side. An enemy force sitting astride the Trigh Capuzzo and Via Balbia would also, of course, cut off significant numbers of Axis troops on the frontier. They could not hold out in the long run if they did not receive regular supplies from Tripoli and Benghazi.

Because of this threat Cruewell was ordered to take the 15th and 21st Panzer Divisions and 'destroy the enemy battle groups in the Bardia–Tobruk–Sidi Omar area'. This was entirely the wrong decision. There was no strong enemy force anywhere near the Trigh Capuzzo. The 3rd RTR and the King's Dragoon Guards had retired back to the position of the rest

Above: A DAK column on the move across open desert. (IWM MH5565)

of the 4th Armoured Brigade late on 19 November, and XIII Corps, who would later push on through this area, were still on the frontier. The 4th Indian Division was deployed to the east of Halfaya, pinning Bach's forces in position, while the 2nd New Zealand Division worked its way slowly round Sidi Omar and into the Axis rear.

As a consequence, DAK's armour spent 20 November chasing shadows, sweeping back and forth across the Trigh Capuzzo and trying to bring to battle a force that did not exist. The 21st Panzer Division finally ran out of fuel ten miles north of Sidi Omar, just north of the vanguard of the 2nd New Zealand Division. It sat there helpless for several hours, fortunately undiscovered by Allied ground forces or aircraft. Finally, resupplied an hour or two after dark, it began to move off westwards to link up with the 15th Panzer Division.

This formation had had a little more success. Late in the afternoon its tanks had run into the lead elements of the 4th Armoured Brigade, who had once more tentatively begun to push northwards across the Trigh el Abd near Gabr Saleh. After a brief fire fight the British Stuarts had again retreated, but to all intents and purposes the two formations were still in contact when darkness fell.

With the Axis armour bottled up at Bir el Gubi or manoeuvring in the desert near the Trigh Capuzzo, the Allies were presented with an opportunity to re-concentrate the 7th Armoured Division at Sidi Rezegh. Unfortunately they did not take it. Gott had initially ordered the 22nd Armoured Brigade to push on from Bir el Gubi to Sidi Rezegh, but on hearing reports from the 4th Armoured Brigade that they were engaging the mass of German armour, he diverted them to join up with the 4th Armoured Brigade at Gabr Saleh. The new orders did not reach the brigade until it was well on its way to linking up with the 7th Armoured Brigade and the Divisional Support Group, and consequently the 22nd Armoured Brigade spent almost the entire day on the move across the desert, engaging no enemy, and not

linking up with the 4th Armoured Brigade until dusk.

The 1st South African Division (only two brigades strong), following in the wake of the 22nd Armoured Brigade, took over the screening of Bir el Gubi, whilst the remaining unit attached to XXX Corps, the 22nd Guards Brigade, was ordered to guard the string of supply dumps now being constructed from Sidi Rezegh back to the frontier.

The weaknesses of the Allied redeployment of 20 November stemmed from the lack of communication between XXX and XIII Corps. The now combined force of the 4th and 22nd Armoured Brigades was intended to stop the German panzers from pushing south across the Trigh el Abd, cutting across the Allied supply line and forcing an abandonment of the offensive to relieve Tobruk. It was still expected, despite all previous battlefield experience, that the Germans would throw wave after wave of tanks at the British armour and that DAK's panzers would be defeated in a set-piece tank-versus-tank battle. Of course, what could have been done was to link up the 4th Armoured Brigade with the 2nd New Zealand Division, and their attached

Below: A PzKpfw III on the move. (IWM MH5852)

1st Army Tank Brigade. This would have provided a flank guard just as strong in terms of tanks, with the addition of significant numbers of infantry and anti-tank guns—more than enough to see off an armoured assault by DAK. This would have left the 22nd Armoured Brigade free to strengthen XXX Corps' forward defences at Sidi Rezegh. However, XXX Corps, which considered itself an élite armoured formation, could not bear to ask its neighbouring 'colonial' infantry for help. This arrogant atti-tude, which was prevalent amongst many senior British tank officers, including those in the 4th Armoured Brigade, would cost them dear. Instead, the 2nd New Zealand Division was left to continue its slow drive towards Sidi Azeiz and Bardia.

Rommel, on hearing that DAK's armour had failed to engage any large enemy force on the 20th, immediately ordered Cruewell to attack the next most significant enemy position, that at Sidi Rezegh. A combined assault by the 15th and 21st

Below: Deception played a major role in the desert campaign, largely because there was a lack of natural cover in which formations could hide from enemy reconnaissance aircraft. Both sides took to creating 'ghost' formations of dummy tanks and trucks, which were then placed out in the desert to mislead the enemy concerning the intentions, strength and true whereabouts of their troops. Here men of a deception unit put the finishing touches to a dummy Stuart light tank, 3 April 1942. (IWM E10145)

Panzer Divisions from the east, and an infantry attack by the Afrika Division, supported by the heavy guns of Artillery Group 104, from the north would be more than enough to defeat the two British brigade-size formations holding the airfield and the ridge line to its south-east. However, the Germans were to face significant problems carrying through their plan.

In the evening of the 20th, Cunningham, pleased with how things were going, decided to launch Operation 'Pop', the planned break-out from Tobruk. This was to begin at dawn the next day, supported by an attack from the 1st Battalion King's Royal Rifle Corps and the 6th RTR northwards from Sidi Rezegh. With only 20 miles between the garrison's forward positions and the airfield, it was hoped that a link-up could be made later that same day.

The attack north from Sidi Rezegh caught the Italian infantry of the Pavia Division, and the German ex-foreign legionnaires of the 361st Infantry Regiment, by surprise. The ridge to the north of the airfield fell to the British quickly, with the loss of only 84 casualties. Over 700 German and Italian prisoners were taken in the assault. A path now lay open from Sidi Rezegh to the rear of the Bologna Infantry Division, holding

Below: Brigadier Willison, Commander of the 32nd Army Tank Brigade, gives instructions to his officers prior to the attempted Tobruk break-out. (IWM E6852)

the sector of the Tobruk siege lines through which the garrison was to attack.

However, the attack by the 32nd Army Tank Brigade and the 70th Infantry Division did not go to plan. The Italian infantry, dug in and well supported by artillery and anti-tank gun fire, put up a much more determined resistance than anticipated. By the end of the day the British had only managed to penetrate half-way through the defence line, and one fortified position in particular, the Tugun emplacement, which overlooked the right flank of the advance, was still firmly in Italian hands. With casualties mounting alarmingly and the number of serviceable Matildas dwindling rapidly, the break-out was called off.

Nevertheless, there still existed a yawning gap to the north of Sidi Rezegh, which, if the British could exploit it quickly, might prove fatal to the Axis' hopes of winning the battle. Rommel, who had driven up to

Above: Unused shells are quickly reloaded on to the tractor half-track of an 88mm gun prior to its relocation on the desert battlefield, the Royal Artillery having just found their range. (IWM HU40330)

coordinate the planned attack of the Afrika Division with the arrival of DAK's panzers, saved the situation. Quickly commandeering four 88mm guns and personally leading the 3rd Reconnaissance Battalion, he plugged the gap between Sidi Azeiz and the Tobruk siege line. The cruisers of the 6th RTR withdrew smartly behind the newly captured ridge as soon as they came under fire from the German anti-tank guns. At the end of the engagement the British held the airfield, the ridge line to its north

and the high ground to its south-east. The Pavia Division was deployed to the north-west of Sidi Rezegh, while the 361st Infantry Regiment of the Afrika Division was positioned to the north-east, the 3rd Reconnaissance Battalion filling the gap between the two formations. The other infantry regiment of the Afrika Division, the 155th, held the high ground at Point 178, to the south-west of the airfield. Hemmed in on three sides, the 7th Armoured Brigade and the 7th Armoured Division Support Group waited for the next German move, hoping that the troops fighting their way out of Tobruk would be with them soon.

Instead of a relief force, the next movement detected outside the Sidi Rezegh perimeter was of panzers moving in from the east. These were the tanks of the 15th and 21st Panzer Divisions, who, following Rommel's orders, were now closing in for the kill. Gott, reasoning that the ap-

Below: British infantry carefully approach an apparently abandoned PzKpfw III Ausf J. Two Bren guns are trained on the open hatches—just in case! (IWM STT110)

proaching tanks could only be a small force since the majority of DAK's panzers were being engaged and destroyed by the 4th and 22nd Armoured Brigades (or so his reports from these formations told him), detached only the 7th Hussars to meet the oncoming armour. These two British armoured brigades, both of which were in contact with the German tanks at dawn on 21 November, could perhaps have done more to prevent the panzer divisions disengaging and moving off to the north-west.

The 4th Armoured Brigade, hampered by the fact that its Stuarts needed refuelling far more often than their German counterparts, quickly fell behind in the pursuit. The 22nd Armoured Brigade, chastened by its drubbing at the hands of Italian anti-tank guns two days previously, declined to become closely engaged with the anti-tank gun screens the Germans deployed to cover their withdrawal. The British units therefore advanced rather cautiously in the

wake of the German panzers, allowing them to strike at Sidi Rezegh unimpeded.

The 7th Hussars never stood a chance. Within an hour of the engagement beginning at the eastern end of the plateau that contained the airfield, the vast majority of the Hussars' tanks were blazing hulks. The panzers pressed on. They now ran into the 25pdr field guns of the Support Group deployed on the approaches to the airfield. Exchanging fire over open sights with the panzers, the guns were knocked out one by one. However, their heavy shells caused considerable losses amongst the German tanks—losses that the outnumbered panzers could ill afford. Just as it appeared that they were about to break through to the aerodrome itself, the German tanks inexplicably withdrew. Gott breathed a sigh of relief.

Cruewell had ordered the retreat because fuel and ammunition had run desperately low and tank losses

had begun to climb dramatically. However, this lull to regroup did not mean the end of tank attacks on Sidi Rezegh. The withdrawal did allow the 7th Armoured Division to concentrate for the first time during the battle, although by this stage considerable losses meant that the formation was a shadow of its former self.

Whilst fighting raged around Sidi Rezegh the 2nd New Zealand Division and 1st Army Tank Brigade had continued with their advance and by the end of 21 November they had crossed the Trigh Capuzzo both east and west of Sidi Azeiz. The 4th Indian Division now began to shift its axis of advance, detaching units and sending them round the Sidi Omar flank of Bach's defences, following in the footsteps of the New Zealanders.

Below: A Matilda tank of the 42nd RTR prepares to move forward in support of the infantry of the 7th Indian Brigade, 24 November 1941. (IWM E3716E)

Above: An Italian 75/46 75mm anti-aircraft gun in action. (IWM STT3313)

Gott had during the day ordered the 5th South African Infantry Brigade to march on Sidi Rezegh from Bir el Gubi. The 1st South African Infantry Brigade was to be ready to follow, and the 22nd Guards Brigade was alerted that it might be needed to contain the Italian forces remaining in the area. The night of 21/22 November passed relatively peacefully for both sides, the German panzers regrouping near Gambut (15th Panzer Division) and Belhamed (21st Panzer Division) while the Allied forces dug in.

As the previous day's direct frontal attack had failed, Rommel and Cruewell devised a more subtle plan which they hoped would evict the British from Sidi Rezegh and turn the tide of battle in their favour. A new attack on the airfield would be opened by the infantry of the 21st Panzer Division striking south from Belhamed towards the ridge now occupied by the King's Royal Rifle Corps. Whilst the Allies' attention was drawn to the northern defensive perimeter, the tanks of the 5th Panzer Regiment would sweep west, then south, and then launch an assault against the western end of Sidi Rezegh plateau. At the same time the 15th Panzer Division was to circle the eastern perimeter and strike at the defences from the south-east.

The attack went as planned. With British attention diverted by German pressure from the north, the tanks of the 5th Panzer Regiment circled the defensive line without being spotted. The first inkling Gott received of an attack from the west was when a large cloud of dust, preceded by some rapidly retreating South African armoured cars, was spotted on the horizon by a member of his own headquarters staff.

Hurriedly turning their 25pdrs to face the panzers, the Support Group were soon engaged at very close range, but the element of surprise had allowed the Germans to close too far for them to be stopped. The Crusaders of the 22nd Armoured Brigade bravely counter-charged the panzers through the gun lines but were driven back, losing 50 per cent of their remaining tanks. The German armour was soon on the airfield itself, the few remaining gun crews and headquarters units retreating back to the south. The infantry of the King's Royal Rifle Corps were now attacked in the rear as well as from the front, and after a short, bloody fire fight the survivors surrendered.

The Germans now controlled all of the British defensive position except for the ridge line to the south-east of the airfield—and even this they were not allowed to hold for long. The 15th

Above: An infantry attack comes to a halt under heavy German shellfire. (IWM E12921)

Panzer Division, arriving on the battlefield just before dusk, crashed into the tanks of the 8th Hussars, part of the 4th Armoured Brigade. Expecting an attack from anywhere but the south, the British tanks were soon dispersed. Luckily night was falling rapidly and not many Stuarts were destroyed by tank fire, but many became lost and in the confusion no one

remembered to tell higher command they were being attacked from the rear.

Worse was to follow. At about 7 p.m. the lead tanks of the 8th Panzer Regiment stumbled across a British unit in leaguer at the base of the ridge. Because the panzers arrived from the south, the British troops assumed they were friendly and no one seems to have given the alarm. The tank commanders simply dismounted and got their crews to shine the panzer headlights on the encamp-

ment. The British troops were caught like startled rabbits. In this way the entire headquarters staff of the 4th Armoured Brigade were ignominiously captured.

The only Allied offensive action of the day had also failed. The 5th South African Brigade, moving up from Bir el Gubi, was ordered to take Point 178, the only section of the southern ridge line still held by Axis troops. The South African infantry were new to desert fighting, and attacking well dug-in German infantry (the hill was held by a battalion of the 155th Infantry Regiment) made the job doubly difficult. The attack went badly wrong from the start. Because of a lack of artillery preparation the Transvaal Scottish Regiment, leading the assault, ran headlong into well-deployed, unsuppressed infantry, with plentiful machine-gun and mortar support. The lead units took heavy casualties and the attack ground to a halt. The South African infantry then spent the rest of the afternoon (the attack had begun at midday) face-down in the baking sun, trying to hug the ground to obtain what little cover there was available. Towards the end of 22 November Gott decided that the Sidi Rezegh area was indefensible and ordered all of his remaining force to pull back into the desert south of the airfield, where they would link up with their transport lines and the as yet relatively unscathed 5th South African Brigade.

Rommel decided that the next day, *Totensonntag* (The Day of the Dead—the German equivalent of Remembrance Sunday), would be a fitting one on which to destroy the remaining Allied formations in the Sidi Rezegh area. The 15th Panzer Division, strengthened by the tanks of the 5th Panzer Regiment, was ordered to sweep south, then west, then to turn and attack the Allied position from the rear. Before the attack began it was to rendezvous with Italian armour from the Ariete Division, which was to push north from Bir el Gubi. These mechanised formations would then drive the Allies back on to the waiting infantry and anti-tank guns of the Afrika and 21st Panzer Divisions, deployed along the ridge to the south of Sidi Rezegh airfield.

The Italian M13/40s found it relatively easy to slip through the covering force at Bir el Gubi (this was now the 22nd Guards Brigade, the 1st South African Brigade having been despatched that morning to support its sister brigade at Sidi Rezegh). After all, the Guards had no tanks and precious few anti-tank guns with which to stop them, so they contented themselves with holding the Italian infantry in position. The Italian armour quickly overtook the South Africans moving northwards, but they were forced to make a wide detour to prevent their becoming embroiled in a fire fight. Because of this they arrived late on the battlefield, taking little part in the final destruction of the 7th Armoured Division and the 5th South African Brigade.

The only other hiccup partially to upset the Axis plan was the sudden appearance of the 6th New Zealand Brigade on the Trigh Capuzzo, east of Sidi Rezegh. Freyberg's 2nd New Zealand Division had wasted no time on reaching the lateral roads and tracks running east to west from the frontier to Tobruk, and by the morning of 23 November the formation was pushing west down the Trigh Capuzzo and Via Balbia with all possible speed. The advance of the New Zealanders was so rapid that it caught the Germans by surprise, and DAK field headquarters was overrun and captured at dawn on the 23rd (fortunately Cruewell was away at the time).

Rommel, who had intended to oversee the armoured attack personally, was caught up in the fighting and spent the whole of the day organising resistance to the New Zealand thrust by redeploying and leading into action the 361st Infantry Regiment and 3rd Reconnaissance Battalion (still with its attached 88s). This brought the 6th New Zealand Brigade's advance to an abrupt halt. Cruewell was therefore left to make the vital battlefield decisions of the day.

The morning of the 23rd was obscured by a thick mist and on its lifting the German armour, moving

Left: New Zealand infantry shepherd prisoners to the rear. A wounded German sits in the back of the Bren Carrier, November 1941. (IWM E3747E)

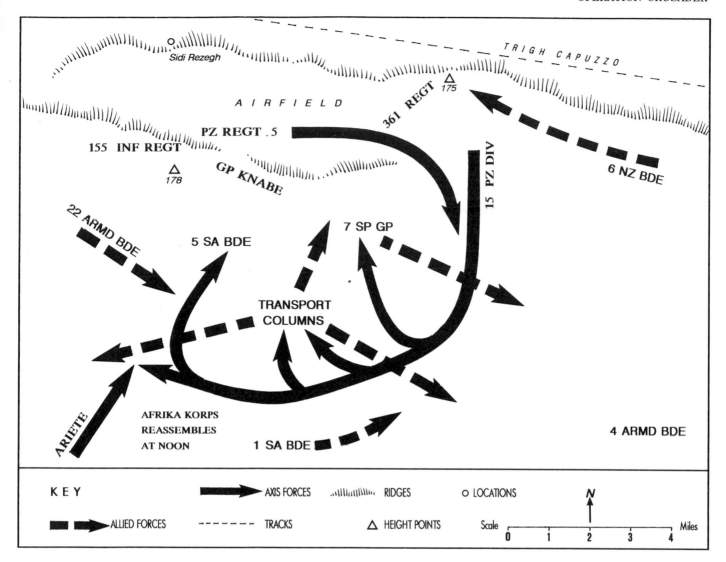

KEY

→ AXIS FORCES   .ₐᵢₗₗₗₗₗₗₗ RIDGES   ○ LOCATIONS

▪▪▪▪▶ ALLIED FORCES   - - - - - TRACKS   △ HEIGHT POINTS   Scale

N

Miles

0 1 2 3 4

south, found itself amongst the transport lines of the 7th Armoured Division, which scattered in all directions on seeing the panzers' approach. A large number of soft vehicles made off to the west, intent on falling back through the 5th South African Brigade defence line to comparative safety. Neumann-Sylkow suggested that the tanks of the 8th Panzer Regiment should follow up these fleeing trucks and attack the South Africans in the confusion that was sure to follow the stampede of soft transport. Cruewell overruled his subordinate: it would be better, he said, to await the arrival of the 5th Panzer Regiment (still making its way forward) and the Italian tanks of the Ariete—they would then be sure to have

enough firepower to overrun the Allied defence line. This was true, but it also gave the Allies time to reorganise in readiness for an attack they were sure would now come from the south-west (at dawn most of the South African Brigade anti-tank guns had been facing northwards, towards Sidi Rezegh). This was to have near-disastrous consequences when the attack finally began at 3 p.m.

With the tanks of the 5th and 8th Panzer Regiments drawn up in a long line and the motorised infantry and artillery of the 15th Panzer Division forming a second echelon, Cruewell ordered the attack against the last remaining Allied defensive position near Sidi Rezegh to begin. The 5th

Above: Operation 'Crusader': victory for DAK at Sidi Rezegh, 23 November 1941.

South African Brigade formed the centre of the Allied line, with the remnants of the 7th Armoured Division Support Group holding the eastern flank and a composite regiment formed from the surviving tanks of the 22nd Armoured Brigade holding the western end of the defence line.

The attack of the German mechanised force, across open desert against Allied troops expecting an assault, was for a time touch-and-go. The Allied tanks, anti-tank guns and field guns destroyed dozens of panzers as they charged their defensive line. South African and British ma-

chine-gun and rifle fire raked the following trucks packed with infantry and caused very heavy casualties, but the Allied defence line was overrun and the remnants of the 7th Armoured Brigade were destroyed (although a number of tanks from the 4th Armoured Brigade did manage to make off into the desert). The South African infantry, devoid of any meaningful tank and artillery support and now surrounded on all sides, surrendered after a heroic resistance. Over 3,000 Allied soldiers were marched off into captivity.

At the end of the day's fighting Rommel felt that he was now close to total victory. If he could turn the defeat of the Allied offensive into a successful attack of his own (as he had with Operation 'Battleaxe'), he might be able to capture a large slice of Egypt—perhaps even Alexandria. To this end, later that night he outlined to his staff a daring plan for a counter-offensive. This foresaw the Afrika Korps pushing on to the frontier defences south of the Sidi Omar Box, trapping the 2nd New Zealand Division and part of the 4th Indian Division in a pocket between Tobruk and Bardia. The remainder of the Indian division would be destroyed on the Sollum–Halfaya front. This would eliminate XIII Corps, and with XXX Corps already destroyed the road into Egypt would be open.

This over-ambitious plan, known to the Allies as 'The Dash to the Wire', would ultimately result in a major

Left, upper: A *Luftwaffe* Heinkel He 111 on its way to bomb rear-area installations in Egypt. (IWM HU70979)
Left, lower: A knocked-out PzKpfw IV, one of its crew lying dead in the foreground, litters the desert battlefield, November 1941. (IWM E6734)
Right: Operation 'Crusader': 'The Dash to the Wire', 24–27 November 1941.

defeat for the Axis forces. Rommel failed to appreciate that Auchinleck was a much more resilient commander than his predecessor, and that he had much more in the way of supplies and reinforcements upon which to draw than had Wavell. Consequently he was not forced into a hurried withdrawal as were the British during 'Battleaxe', and the Allied formations in the field were not frightened into a stampede to the rear just by the movement of two depleted panzer divisions across their flank. And this was the crux of the matter. Whereas Rommel in 'Battleaxe' commanded an outflanking force superior in every way to its opponents, this was not so during 'The Dash to the Wire'.

At the end of 23 November DAK had only 90 tanks left in operational order (72 had been lost in the battle with the 5th South African Brigade). The 1st Army Tank Brigade, accompanying the 2nd New Zealand Division, still had over 100 Matildas in the field; and the 32nd Army Tank Brigade in Tobruk could sortie again with roughly the same number of vehicles. Even the decimated 7th Armoured Division, the survivors of which had retreated south into the desert, could still field a composite battalion of 30-plus tanks (mostly Stuarts from the 4th Armoured Brigade). There was, therefore, in Auchinleck's eyes, no need to panic—yet.

Rommel easily convinced himself that XXX Corps had been utterly de-

stroyed as a fighting force. But, as has already been stated, within one or two days the 7th Armoured Division was putting composite units into the field, the 1st South African Infantry Brigade was untouched and so was the 22nd Guards Brigade at Bir el Gubi. These formations continued to operate west of the frontier even after DAK reached Sidi Omar, and they were one of the reasons Rommel was eventually forced into a strategic withdrawal.

Rommel's forces (Mussolini had ordered Bastico to hand over operational control of all Italian forces in the theatre for the duration of the battle on the 23rd) had performed magnificently, destroying over three times as many tanks as they had

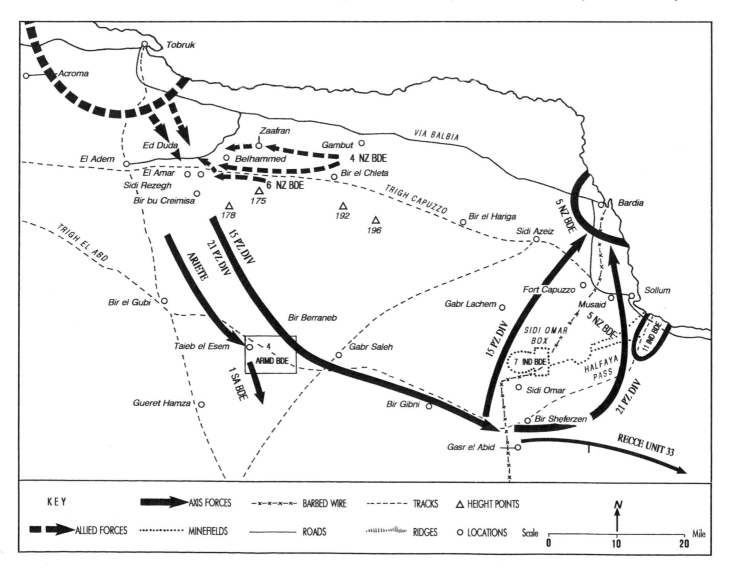

KEY — AXIS FORCES — x—x—x— BARBED WIRE — - - - - TRACKS — △ HEIGHT POINTS — N

— ALLIED FORCES — MINEFIELDS — ROADS — RIDGES — ○ LOCATIONS — Scale 0 10 20 Mile

themselves lost and capturing thousands of Allied prisoners, but this was still not enough to offset the massive Allied superiority in numbers of men and equipment.

In the early hours of 24 November Rommel issued the orders for his counter offensive. DAK, under his personal command, was to drive towards the frontier, relieve the Bardia and Halfaya garrisons and effectively pocket the 2nd New Zealand Division against the coast. The Trieste Division was ordered to move up to the Tobruk perimeter where the last British sortie had been made, to strengthen the positions of the depleted Bologna Division. RECAM was ordered forward to patrol the area between Bir el Gubi and Sidi Rezegh, to mop up any remaining operational units of the 7th Armoured Division in the locality. However, as the backbone of the formation was three paramilitary units, two battalions of Fascist Blackshirt infantry and a single Caribineri battalion, none of which had ever before seen combat, it is not surprising that they failed utterly to hold the Allied formations in check.

Rommel not only underestimated the effectiveness of the remaining units of XXX Corps still operating in the desert (the 7th Armoured Division began to receive replacement tanks and tank crews within 48 hours of their supposed destruction at Sidi Rezegh), but he also refused to believe that XIII Corps could stay in the field in the face of renewed pressure from the Axis. The order to the 3rd Reconnaissance Battalion of the 21st Panzer Division exemplifies this. It was told to push down the Via Balbia

Left, upper: Italian FIAT tractors with 75mm portee field guns on the move. (IWM HU28377)
Left, lower: An Italian Fascist Blackshirt Militia 47-32 anti-tank gun in action. (IWM HU28396A)

towards Bardia—an extraordinary order. A single battalion, even with an attached battery of 88mm guns, stood no chance whatsoever of any appreciable advance against an entire enemy division. Rommel's over-confidence was soon to take a major blow that would finally shake him out of his self-delusion.

At 10.30 p.m. on 24 November, with Rommel at their head, the 15th and 21st Panzer Divisions set off for the Egyptian/Libyan border. Late that afternoon he reached the frontier, with DAK stretched out behind him over 40 miles of desert. This sudden advance temporarily threw XXX Corps into complete disorder, and panic set in at 8th Army Headquarters. Cunningham declared that he was going to order a complete withdrawal, for both XXX and XIII Corps. Fortunately for the Allies, this move, which would have proved disastrous, was countermanded by Auchinleck, who had just arrived at 8th Army HQ to observe the latest developments at first hand.

Auchinleck, who even before arriving at the front had begun to harbour serious doubts about Cunningham's effectiveness as an army commander, decided to relieve him of his position. He was not particularly enamoured of the performances of the corps commanders in the field either, so promoting one of them to take over was out of the question. He therefore decided to turn over command of the 8th Army to his Deputy Chief of Staff, General Neil Ritchie, effective from 26 November.

Rommel had expected to run into the main body of the 4th Indian Division working its way round the southern flank of the frontier defences, but instead his armoured column hit fresh air. Pressing on across the frontier, Rommel and Cruewell and their immediate staffs lost their way and were forced to spend the night of 24/25 November camped out

in hostile territory. Fortunately they were not discovered by any Allied patrols and were able to find their way back to the main body of DAK next morning.

Rommel's frustration at getting lost, compounded by the fact that DAK had not contacted any Allied troop concentrations in the open desert, led him to order the 5th Panzer Regiment to assault the only known enemy position within immediate striking distance, the 7th Indian Brigade at Sidi Omar. While the attack was in progress the remainder of the 15th Panzer Division were to work their way northwards, around the western side of the Indian brigade's defensive box, bringing them, it was hoped, into contact with other associated units of the 4th Indian Division. Meanwhile the 21st

Above: Air Vice-Marshal Sir Arthur Conningham (left), Commander-in-Chief of the Desert Air Force, discusses the strategic situation with the 8th Army commander, Lieutenant-General Sir Neil Ritchie (centre, with pipe) and one of his staff, Brigadier A. Galloway, at 8th Army Forward Headquarters, 10 December 1941. (IWM E7000)

Panzer Division was to sweep the area between Sidi Omar and Halfaya Pass in the hope of a similar contact. Unfortunately for Rommel, the only other formation in contact with Bach's defensive force was the 11th Indian Brigade, who were deployed below the Halfaya escarpment and thus evaded detection.

The 21st Panzer Division spent a fruitless day moving back and forth across their allotted patrol area, being bombed occasionally by roving RAF aircraft. The 15th Panzer Division did not do much better, only managing to overrun and destroy the rear-area workshops of the 1st Army Tank Brigade late that afternoon. The 5th Panzer Regiment ended the day wishing they had not found the enemy either. Their attack on the dug-in 7th Indian Brigade was a costly failure. Protected by German-laid minefields which funnelled the attacking panzers into prepared killing grounds for the brigade's 2pdr anti-tank guns, they lost over half their remaining tank strength—panzers Rommel could ill afford to lose. Out of luck and almost out of fuel, DAK finished the day where it had started. Rommel's next move was shaped not by his plans but by a forced reaction to Freyberg's aggressive New Zealanders.

Whilst DAK had wandered fruitlessly in the desert, the 2nd New Zealand Division had pushed on towards Tobruk. As the day went on the 361st Infantry Regiment of the Afrika Division came under more and more pressure in their defensive positions west of Sidi Rezegh from the infantry of the 4th and 6th New Zealand Infantry Brigades and Matildas of the 1st Army Tank Brigade. Frantic signals were sent from Panzergruppe

Right, top: Tanks of the 21st Panzer Division on the move near Sollum during the final phase of Rommel's 'Dash to the Wire', November 1941. (IWM MH5588)
Right, centre: The crew of a Matilda, captured and used by the Germans, surrenders to New Zealand infantry, 3 December 1941. The tank had been knocked out by another Matilda in service with the British! (IWM E3744E)
Right, bottom: South African infantry move forward against an Italian position through a smokescreen, 28 November 1941. (IWM E6772)

Afrika Headquarters to Rommel stating that the front could not be held for much longer and that DAK's armour was desperately needed. These, however, did not reach him until 26 November. At the same time the Ariete Armoured Division, which had been ordered forward to the frontier to support DAK, was soundly rebuffed at Taieb el Esem on the Trigh el Abd by the combined efforts of the 1st South African Infantry Brigade and the remnants of the 4th Armoured Brigade.

Rommel, on receiving the portents of disaster from the Tobruk area, decided that he still had a little time to try to locate and destroy the Allied force in the frontier area. Consequently the 15th and 21st Panzer Divisions spent the day manoeuvring to the west of the Halfaya defensive positions, the 21st Panzer Division attacking and capturing the positions held by elements of the 5th New Zealand Brigade near Fort Capuzzo. That evening both divisions retired to the Bardia perimeter, where they were replenished from the garrison's supply stocks.

Unfortunately for Rommel, his calculation that the Afrika Division could hold out for another 24 hours was incorrect. On 26 November the New Zealanders pushed forward and

Right, upper: Axis prisoners shelter in fox-holes near Tobruk before being taken to the rear. (IWM E6914)
Right, lower: The Tobruk link-up, Ed Duda, 26 November 1941. Left to right: Major 'Stump' Gibbon (44 RTR), Captain Humphreys (4 RTR), Lieutenant-Colonel O'Carrol (OC 4 RTR), Major J. Holden (4 RTR), Brigadier Willison (32nd Army Tank Brigade), Lieutenant-Colonel F. Brown (OC 1 RTR) and unknown New Zealand infantry officer (in tin hat). The Matilda nearest the camera is O'Carrol's tank, while the Mk VI parked behind it belongs to Brown. (IWM E6898)

captured Belhamed. At the same time the 70th Division launched another attack against the Tobruk perimeter, now held by the Trieste Division. After heavy fighting the British broke through and the garrison were able to capture the escarpment at Ed Duda. The two Allied forces then linked up in the vicinity of the Axis-built Tobruk by-pass. Technically Tobruk had been relieved. The Allied position now lay in a long corridor from Tobruk to Point 175 east of Sidi Rezegh, taking in Ed Duda, Belhamed, Zaafron, Sidi Rezegh, its airfield and its surrounding escarpments.

Below: Crusader tanks of the Royal Gloucestershire Hussars prepare to move forward during Operation 'Crusader', 26 November 1941. (IWM E6724)

At dawn on 27 November Rommel, finally realising the seriousness of the situation to his west, ordered the 15th and 21st Panzer Divisions to advance along the Trigh Capuzzo as fast as they could to hit the New Zealanders in the rear. This move began well with the 8th Panzer Regiment overrunning and capturing the headquarters of the 5th New Zealand Brigade at Sidi Azeiz. However, Ritchie was well aware of the possibility of a panzer attack on Freyberg from the east. He ordered the 4th and 22nd Armoured Brigades, which had spent most of the last four days reorganising, having received substantial reinforcements of men and tanks, to push north and hit the advancing panzers in the flank.

The two armoured formations clashed near Bir el Chleta in the late afternoon, some eight miles east of the New Zealand defensive positions. At dusk, after two hours of heavy fighting, the British tanks withdrew to the south to leaguer for the night, enabling the Germans to claim a victory. However, battlefield losses had been roughly equal—losses the Germans could not afford. The delay to the panzer advance caused by the fighting also gave the New Zealanders time to organise a defensive perimeter to the north, east and south of their headquarters near Sidi Rezegh (the western flank of their position was covered by the 70th Division).

November 28 saw little in the way of action, Rommel spending most of the day reacquainting himself with the situation at Panzergruppe HQ (having flown there first thing in the morning) and organising his forces for an attack the next day. The men

Right, upper: Holding Sidi Rezegh Ridge, 29 November 1941. (IWM E6863)
Right, lower: British infantry drop prone as they come under renewed shelling near Sidi Rezegh, 1 December 1941. (IWM E6890)

of the 2nd New Zealand and 70th Divisions dug in deeper and waited for the assault to come, hoping that relief from an outside force would not be too long in arriving. The once again depleted 4th and 22nd Armoured Brigades did try a few tentative attacks towards Sidi Rezegh from the south but were relatively easily beaten off.

Both sides were now beginning to feel the effects of ten days of continuous combat: troops were exhausted, equipment was worn to breaking point and losses had turned once-strong fighting formations into barely viable battlefield units. Despite this, Rommel was determined to encircle and destroy the New Zealanders, thereby isolating the Tobruk garrison once more. This, he hoped, would force Ritchie to conclude that Operation 'Crusader' had failed and that a withdrawal to the frontier to reorganise and re-equip was the most sensible option open to him.

For the assault on the New Zealanders Rommel prepositioned the 21st Panzer Division at the eastern end of the Sidi Rezegh position, with the Ariete Division covering the southern approaches and elements of the Afrika Division covering the northern perimeter. The 15th Panzer Division was ordered to move around the southern flank of the 2nd New Zealand Division and then to turn northwards, through the defensive positions held by the Trieste Division, to drive a wedge between the New Zealanders and the 70th Division at Ed Duda. At the same time the 21st Panzer Division would attack the Sidi Rezegh position from the east.

Unfortunately for Rommel the attack did not go as planned. Both the Ariete and 21st Panzer Divisions were attacked from the south by the 7th Armoured Division and the lead elements of the 1st South African Brigade. Although the attacks were not pressed with much vigour, enough pressure was applied to thwart the 21st Panzer Division's plan of attack. The situation was made worse when the division's commanding officer, General Johann von Ravenstein, was captured by New Zealand infantry whilst on forward reconnaissance, leaving the division leaderless for several crucial hours. The attack by the 15th Panzer Divi-

77

Right: The war in North Africa was notable for the chivalrous behaviour of both sides. Here a captured German doctor tends wounded British infantrymen at an Allied Forward Dressing Station, 28 November 1941. (IWM E6795)

sion initially went well. Sweeping through the lines of the Trieste Division, the German panzers took the British defenders by surprise and captured the Ed Duda escarpment. However, that night the 70th Division mounted a strong, well coordinated counter-attack and the infantry of the 115th Rifle Regiment were forced back on to the supporting Italian infantry of the Trieste Division.

Still Rommel would not give up. The 15th Panzer Division was moved to a new position south of the New Zealanders' Sidi Rezegh defences, where their depleted strength was reinforced by the addition of infantry and artillery elements from the 21st Panzer Division. The next morning the formation struck north, whilst battle groups from the Afrika Division pinned the New Zealand infantry in position around the other edges of the perimeter, stopping Freyberg from reinforcing his southern flank. The 7th Armoured Division tried to intervene but were beaten off by

tanks from the Ariete Division and the 5th Panzer Regiment.

The assault was a success. By the end of the day the airfield and the ridge line south of Sidi Rezegh were in German hands, despite a counter-attack by the infantry of the 1st South African Brigade against Point 175, which was defeated with relative ease. During the day's fighting the 15th Panzer Division had managed to break into the heart of Freyberg's defences and capture 600

men and two batteries of 25pdr guns. That night Freyberg decided that his position, surrounded on three sides, with only a very narrow corridor connecting him with the Tobruk garrison and with German forces threatening to split his position in half, was untenable. He reluctantly gave orders for the remaining units of his command to break out to the southeast the following morning. This they successfully managed to do, but another four batteries of guns and a further 1,000 men were taken prisoner. The 2nd New Zealand Division, along with the 7th Armoured Division and the 1st South African Brigade, then moved off southwards into

Left: An Italian soldier walks past a knocked-out PzKpfw IV to give himself up to an Indian infantryman, 8 December 1941. (IWM E3768E)
Right, upper: An Indian Bren Carrier passes a burning PzKpfw III, 2 December 1941. (IWM E6924)
Right, lower: British troops search Axis bunkers near Tobruk for enemy stragglers, December 1941. (IWM E7202)

the desert to regroup and receive reinforcements. The garrison of Tobruk was once again isolated. It seemed as though Rommel had beaten Ritchie, and that Operation 'Crusader' had failed.

However, DAK's latest success had been a pyrrhic victory, although it took Rommel until 4 December fully to realise the fact. The German divisions, along with the best Italian formations, the Trieste and Ariete Divisions, had been severely weakened by two weeks of heavy fighting. Rommel did not have the same ac-

cess to replacement vehicles and reinforcements as did the Allies, and all these units were now operating at 50 per cent or less of their establishment strengths. The remaining Italian infantry divisions, although not as badly hit by losses, could not be trusted to hold ground without effective armoured support. Almost totally lacking in transport, they could quite easily be outmanoeuvred by the motorised Allied formations and destroyed, as had happened to the Italian 10th Army in the winter of 1940/41.

Top: Infantry of the 29th Indian Brigade assault Italian defensive positions at Jalo, 5/6 December 1941. (IWM E3758E)
Above: A Matilda passes a knocked-out PzKpfw II, December 1941. (IWM E6903)

On 3 and 4 December Rommel ordered detachments of the Afrika Korps to advance on Bardia to open up a supply route to his cut-off frontier defences. However, the advance was effectively repulsed, the returning troops declaring that even more Allied units seemed to be pouring into

Cyrenaica. This was the 4th Indian Division, now moving forward to link up with the 22nd Guards Brigade, their position on the frontier having been taken over by the 2nd South African Division newly arrived from Alexandria. With the appearance of a large, fresh Allied formation to his front and disquieting news about an enemy force (E Force—the 29th Indian Brigade and the 6th and 7th South African Armoured Car Regiments) of unknown size moving to outflank him through the deep desert, Rommel decided to pull back

and leave Tobruk firmly in Allied hands.

At first he felt that all that was needed was a very limited withdrawal to a new defensive position south of Gazala (this position had been fortified by Italian rear-echelon troops earlier in the year for just such an eventuality). To cover this withdrawal the Ariete, 15th and 21st Panzer Divisions pushed south-east towards Bir el Gubi. Here they contacted the tanks of the 7th Armoured Division and the lead elements of the 4th Indian Division and held them

Above: A rather dubious picture! An Italian M13/40 tank crewman surrenders to a British soldier south-west of Gazala, 22 December 1941. However, as the infantryman has no bayonet fixed, and wears no webbing or equipment, the chances are that the cooperative POW is re-enacting his capture earlier missed by the cameraman. (IWM E7304)

at bay while the foot-slogging Italian infantry disengaged from the Tobruk perimeter and retreated westwards. During the night of 7/8 December the Axis armour and motorised infantry

81

broke away from the enemy and fell back to cover the southern flank of the new Gazala position.

The next day Rommel despatched the Afrika Division to Agedabia, 100 miles south of Benghazi, to guard against the advance of E Force, who had captured Jalo and were now threatening to thrust northwards and cut the Axis line of communication with Tripoli. General Max Summerman, their commanding officer, would not be going with them. He had been severely wounded several days previously and died on 10 December. General Neumann-

Below: : Indian Sikh infantry rest during the advance on Derna, December 1941. (IWM E7254)

Sylkow, commander of the 15th Panzer Division, had been similarly wounded by shellfire on 7 December. He died on the day his division took up its new defensive position south of Gazala. Rommel had lost all three of his senior field commanders within eleven days.

By the time the 7th Armoured Division, the 2nd New Zealand Division (now with the 1st South African Brigade under command), the 4th Indian Division (plus the 22nd Guards Brigade) and the 1st Army Tank Brigade had organised themselves for an assault on the new position it was 11 December. The attacks, which began on the 11th and lasted until the 15th, were not pressed too hard: the Allied units (except for the Indians) were se-

verely battered, tired to the point of exhaustion and low on fuel and ammunition. Nevertheless Rommel came to realise that his troops, particularly the Italian contingent, were in an even worse state. There was no way he was going to hold on to his new position, even with attacks made in a half-hearted manner. His troops were dead on their feet and virtually out of ammunition, fuel and food. Morale was low, particularly amongst his Italian troops, and he was now outnumbered by at least four to one in tanks (for example the revitalised 4th Armoured Brigade could boast 136 Stuarts at the end of 'Crusader', more than the entire total that Panzergruppe Afrika, including Italian vehicles, could muster). It was

clear that another retreat was necessary. This would have to be a major withdrawal, far enough to enable Panzergruppe Afrika to re-form unmolested.

On 15 December Rommel announced his intention to pull back to the Mersa el Brega bottleneck, thus abandoning Cyrenaica to the Allies. General Bastico, nominally Rommel's superior, initially forbade the retreat; Cavallero, the Italian Chief of Staff, concurred with his colleague's judgement. But when Rommel presented them with a full picture of Axis losses and the almost total lack of supplies and reinforcements and asked them to come up with an alternative plan of action, they could not.

The retreat was carried out with great skill. Throughout DAK's principal opponent was the RAF, the 8th Army having been fought virtually to a standstill. Rommel's main concern was that an Allied motorised or mechanised column would cut across the base of the Cyrenaica bulge and cut off the Italian infantry division's line of retreat, so it was a great relief when the 15th Panzer Division manoeuvred into position south of Benghazi on 20 December. Fortunately for DAK a tank transport had arrived in Benghazi on 17 December and the 15th Panzer Division's battlefield strength increased to 40 panzers.

On 23 December the 7th Armoured Division, in the van of the Allied pursuit, tried to cut the Via Balbia between Benghazi and Agedabia but instead ran headlong into the well-deployed tanks of the 15th Panzer Division. The British, strung out across the desert in a ragged line, committed their tanks to action piecemeal and were easily rebuffed. The next day, with the Italian infantry columns now comparatively safe, Benghazi was evacuated and DAK pulled back to Agedabia.

On 26 December the British carried out their last attack of Operation 'Crusader' when tanks of the 7th Armoured Division tried to break through the German defensive position at Agedabia. However, the British tank brigades, short of experienced crews and in dire need of a long respite for reorganisation and re-equipment, did not put up a good showing. When on 28 December Rommel launched a limited counter-attack with DAK's panzers (now about 70 vehicles in total), the British armour suffered very heavy losses and was thrown back in confusion. Shortly thereafter the 7th Armoured Division was withdrawn to a position south of Tobruk to rest and refit.

Rommel, aware that the Agedabia defensive position, although strong, was not unassailable, pulled back once more to the narrow Mersa el Brega bottleneck on 5 January 1942. He was now back defending the position where his DAK troops had first seen action against the British some nine months earlier.

Right, upper: Sikh troops of the Allied advance guard de-bus in Derna and fan out to search for enemy rearguard positions, December 1941. (IWM E7361) Right, lower: Who said the Germans had no sense of humour? A sign left behind in a Benghazi hotel wishing the British advance guard a Happy Christmas and promising that the Germans would be back (which of course they were). 6 January 1942. (IWM E7575)

CHAPTER FIVE

OPERATION 'THESEUS'

By 11 January 1942 Panzergruppe Afrika had concentrated in the Mersa el Brega position. Although it was seriously understrength, its strategic position was not unfavourable. The German defensive position virtually precluded any large-scale outflanking manoeuvre: if the Allies attacked it would be head-on against well dug-in troops. Two large supply convoys had arrived in Tripoli on 18 December and 5 January, bringing with them large stocks of fuel, ammunition and four companies of replacement panzers. Being nearer Tripolitania, DAK was assured of much greater *Luftwaffe* and *Regia Aero-*

nautica support, and the transfer of Luftflotte 2 to Sicily and the subsequent battering it began to give to Malta meant that the number of supply convoys getting through was increasing dramatically.

In contrast, the 8th Army was thinly stretched out across Cyrenaica with a long line of communications trailing back into Egypt. Conversely, the RAF were not able to support the Allied formations furthest forward as well as they wished, owing to a lack of range on their fighters and a paucity of forward airfields. For the first seventeen days of 1942 Ritchie also faced the problem of substantial Axis forces still sitting astride his main

line of communication, the Via Balbia. Bach's mixed Italian-German Kampfgruppe still held the Halfaya Pass, and the port of Bardia, strongly fortified, continued as a large Axis garrison. It took over two weeks (Bardia fell on 2 January and Halfaya on 17 January) to mop up this behind-the-lines resistance, and the operation fully engaged the 2nd South African Division and the Matildas of the 1st and 32nd Army Tank Brigades. At the end of the fighting the Allies had captured a further 13,800 Axis prisoners, including the now famous Major Reverend Wilhelm Bach.

While Ritchie was preoccupied with eliminating the troublesome Axis forces in his rear, Rommel was busy planning a riposte that would have the Allies once again running for the frontier. From intelligence sources (mainly his extremely effective wireless intercept service) Rommel was able to ascertain that the 7th Armoured Division had been pulled back and that its place in the front line had been taken by the 1st Armoured Division, a formation with no combat or desert experience, fresh from England. Not only that, but the division was also one brigade short (the 22nd Armoured Brigade had

Left: *Regia Aeronautica* **Fiat BR.20M medium bombers on a desert runway. (IWM HU70993)**

Above: South African infantry cautiously shepherd surrendering Germans from their defensive position near Bardia, 2 January 1942. (IWM E7456)
Right: An Italian prisoner carries his wounded friend to the rear after the fall of Bardia, 2 January 1942. (IWM E7540)

originally been earmarked for the 1st Armoured Division but had been committed to 'Crusader' as part of the 7th Armoured Division and had been withdrawn with them). The division now consisted of the 2nd Armoured Brigade and the 1st Support Group.

The 4th Indian Division was present in the Benghazi area, well behind the leading 1st Armoured Division units (Rommel suspected poor Allied deployment but in fact the division was marooned there because of a lack of fuel and transport). The 1st South African Division, 2nd New Zealand Division and 70th Infantry

Left, upper: Italian Army and Navy prisoners file to the rear after the surrender of Bardia, 2 January 1942. The port blazes in the background. (IWM E7553)
Left, lower: South African infantry clear out houses in the Sollum area still held by Axis troops, 19 January 1942. (IWM E7709)
Right: The Reverend Major Wilhelm Bach (left), hero of Halfaya, Major-General Schmidt (centre) and Major-General Johann von Ravenstein, the three prize captives of early 1942, leave the Cairo hotel where they were temporarily held to go for a drive, 25 January 1942. (IWM E7850)
Below: South African infantry look down on Sollum from a former Axis position on top of the escarpment, 19 January 1942. (IWM E7689)

Division appeared not to be in western Cyrenaica at all (German intelligence was correct: all three battered formations had been withdrawn to recuperate and refit). The only formation of which Rommel did not know the whereabouts was the 201st Guards Brigade (newly formed from the nucleus of the 22nd Guards Brigade), which was based at Agedabia.

With 117 German and 79 Italian tanks now at his disposal, Rommel felt that if he struck quickly he might even be able to obtain local battlefield superiority (he was right: the 1st Armoured Division could only muster a total of 150 tanks). The gathering of sufficient supplies and transport for the counter-offensive was the most serious obstacle to be overcome, but after a week of commandeering fuel and trucks from units not participating in the thrust Rommel felt he was

Below: Operation 'Theseus', 21 January–4 February 1942.

ready. Orders were issued to divisional commanders in the evening of 19 January. The attack, codenamed Operation 'Theseus', was to begin at 6.30 p.m. on the 21st.

The assault was made by two main battle groups. Kampfgruppe Marcks, consisting of the mobile elements of the 90th Light Division (as the Afrika Division was now known), and a detachment of tanks from the 5th Panzer Regiment pushed along the Via Balbia, while the remainder of DAK (15th and 21st Panzer Divisions) advanced through the desert to the north of Wadi el Faregh. The Italian XX Corps (Ariete and Trieste Divisions) followed in the wake of Kampfgruppe Marcks, ready to exploit any fractures that might appear in the Allied defence line. Werner Marcks, previously in command of the 155th Rifle Regiment, now commanded the 90th Light Division, whilst the 15th Panzer Division was now led by General Gustav von

Vaerst and the 21st Panzer Division by General Georg von Bismarck.

At first the advance went well, the tanks of the 8th Panzer Regiment overrunning and capturing several British trucks and 25pdr field guns of the 1st Armoured Division Support Group which had become bogged down in soft sand in their eagerness to get away from the advancing panzers. After dark on the 21st Rommel received air reconnaissance reports that the 1st Armoured Division was attempting to concentrate for a stand south and east of Agedabia. To counter this he decided to take personal command of Kampfgruppe Marcks and drive with all speed up the Via Balbia through Agedabia and on to Antelat and Saunnu. This would effectively turn the right flank of the 1st Armoured Division. The 15th and 21st Panzer Divisions were to follow Rommel up the main coast road. The leading German units captured Agedabia,

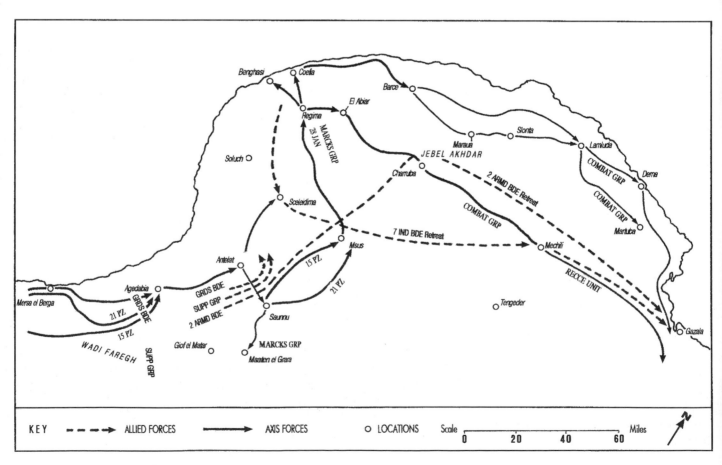

KEY   – – – → ALLIED FORCES   ——→ AXIS FORCES   ○ LOCATIONS   Scale   0   20   40   60   Miles

Right, top: German infantry on the move during Operation 'Theseus', January 1942. (IWM HU5589)
Right, centre: A sIG 33 auf Fgst PzKpfw II (a 150mm self-propelled gun based on the PzKpfw II chassis) of Panzer Unit 707 moves forward during Operation 'Theseus' shortly after the unit's arrival in North Africa. (IWM HU66479)
Right, bottom: A DAK 88mm FlaK gun moves forward during Operation 'Theseus', January 1942. (IWM MH5833)

after encountering little resistance, at 11 a.m. on 22 January. Kampfgruppe Marcks pushed on quickly and was in Antelat by 3.30 p.m.

The sluggishness of the 1st Armoured Division's reaction to this move was exacerbated by the fact that the formation had chosen to concentrate in the open desert. The Division's Support Group, all lorry-borne infantry or truck-towed artillery, was much slower moving across the difficult terrain of the area than if it would have been had it been deployed on or near the coast road. Consequently Marcks's motorised formations were able to maintain a much higher speed on the metalled highway, even against limited opposition, than were the trucks of the 1st Armoured Division Support Group, who, on hearing that they had been outflanked, struggled to race to the rear as fast as they could.

Rommel's plan was to form a cordon with the 15th and 21st Panzer Divisions running from Agedabia–Antelat–Saunnu, thus hemming in the 1st Armoured Division and the 201st Guards Brigade from the north and west. The Italian XX Corps were ordered to deploy just south of the Via Balbia and to sweep any remaining British forces towards a pocket, the third side of which would be formed by Kampfgruppe Marcks moving south from Saunnu. Unfortunately, this audacious attempt to entrap the

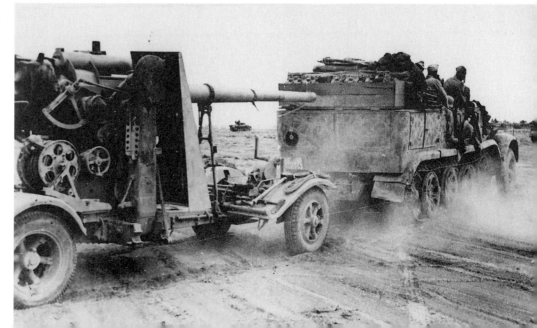

1st Armoured Division and 201st Guards Brigade failed, owing not to an effective British counterstroke but to an oversight on the part of staff officers at Rommel's HQ. The units from the 21st Panzer Division that were to take over the garrisoning of Saunnu did not receive their instructions to do so until after Kampfgruppe Marcks had pushed on into the open desert. Units from the 1st Armoured Division found the gap in the Axis cordon and the majority of them managed to slip through. Unfortunately Rommel did not realise it and DAK spent 24 January scouring the area for the armour he was sure he had trapped. Even though the vast majority of the 2nd Armoured Brigade got away, significant amounts of soft transport and artillery pieces were captured.

In the evening of 24 January Rommel decided to advance towards Msus the next day and, he hoped, bring to contact the retreating armour of the 1st Armoured Division. General Sir Frank Messervy, now in command of the 1st Armoured Division, had decided, roughly at the same time, to turn and make a stand some six miles north-west of Saunnu. Msus contained the 8th Army's forward supply depot, and he feared that if Rommel captured it intact it could be used as a springboard from which he could repeat his famed offensive of the previous April. However, if the 1st Armoured Division could hold DAK at bay, then with

Left, top: British prisoners captured during Rommel's Cyrenaica counter-offensive wait to be shipped out from Benghazi, February 1942. (IWM MH5857) Left, centre: Transport and tanks of the 15th Panzer Division on the move, January 1942. (IWM MH5828) Left, bottom: Captured troops from the 4th Indian Division march through Benghazi, January 1942. (IWM MH5555)

reinforcements there was a possibility that the enemy could be pushed back to his start line.

Unfortunately for Messervy, the troops under his command were not up to the task. All that was needed was a well coordinated attack from the 8th Panzer Regiment, supported by artillery fire and fast-moving anti-tanks guns, and the British front shattered. The tank crews of the 2nd Armoured Brigade, untried in desert combat, turned and fled at the first sign of panzer pressure, taking their supporting infantry and artillery with them, turning a shambolic defence into a mass rout. The German mechanised columns had a field day, weaving in and out of the fleeing British units, shooting up armour and transport at their leisure. The British were too concerned with getting away to put up any form of coherent resistance. After covering 50 miles in under four hours, the 15th Panzer Division broke off the pursuit when they overran the Msus supply dumps.

Rommel hoped to refuel from captured petrol stocks and continue the pursuit across the base of the Jebel Akhdar as he had done the previous year. He was to be disappointed. The Msus dumps, although they held hundreds of tons of useful supplies, contained very little petrol: someone with foresight had destroyed much of the stock before DAK's arrival. There was not enough fuel to enable a pursuing force of sufficient size to stay on the tail of the 1st Armoured Division, now heading flat-out for Mechili.

Right, upper: Pro-Italian Arabs demonstrate their loyalty to Mussolini and Hitler after the recapture of Benghazi during Operation 'Theseus'. (IWM MH5879) Right, lower: A German infantryman digs in at DAK's new positions near Gazala, February 1942. (IWM MH5834)

However, Ritchie did not realise just how short of fuel DAK was and suspected, even hoped, that Rommel would try a re-run of the previous year's offensive. The German commander was, however, not so easy to read. Deciding against a thrust across the base of the Cyrenaican peninsula, he instead planned to attack Benghazi, where he suspected an even bigger Allied supply dump was located (the end of the Msus pursuit had seen 96 tanks, 38 guns and 190 lorries, along with hundreds of tons of food, cigarettes and beer, fall into Rommel's hands).

The 15th and 21st Panzer Divisions were ordered to make a feint towards Mechili, which would, it was hoped, convince Ritchie and Godwin-

Above: General Ugo Cavallero, the Italian Chief of Staff, leaves a briefing in Benghazi after a tour of the Axis front line, March 1942. (IWM HU32704)
Left: Vital reinforcements for the 8th Army: a ship carrying Grant and Stuart tanks is unloaded at Alexandria, 13 March 1942. (IWM E9224)

Austen, the corps commander left in charge of Cyrenaica operations, that an attack from this direction was imminent. Meanwhile Rommel, once again in personal command of Kampfgruppe Marcks, would lead them north through the foothills of the Jebel Akhdar, then turn west and attack Benghazi. The Italian XX Corps would push up the Via Balbia at the same time to make a frontal attack on the port.

The feint worked. Ritchie ordered his remaining armour and all the other reinforcements he could scrape together to concentrate at Mechili. Confident that with Rommel splitting his force his tanks stood a good chance of defeating the German panzers in a defensive positional battle, he sat back and waited. Godwin-Austen, concerned that Ritchie was ignoring the possibility of an Axis thrust up the coast road to Benghazi, requested permission to withdraw the 4th Indian Division at least to a line parallel to that forming at Mechili. Ritchie refused. The Indians, he felt, should be able to hold any secondary thrust made by the few German units now left in the Msus area (he conveniently ignored the fact

Right: Two men of a Cypriot Pioneer Company keep a look out for enemy aircraft while their compatriots build field fortifications, 28 February 1942. (IWM E8947)
Below: A burnt-out PzKpfw III. This one was destroyed by a direct hit from an artillery shell, 6 March 1942. (IWM E9088)

93

that two Italian divisions, one of them armoured, were accompanying the German counter-offensive). He also failed to take into account the fact that the 4th Indian Division was stretched out along the Cyrenaican coastline from Benghazi to Maraua, and only the 7th Indian Brigade was in a position to make a stand to defend the port.

Thus Rommel's surprise attack on Benghazi from the Jebel Akhdar, launched during torrential rain on 28 January, could quite easily have resulted in the rapid destruction of at least one Indian brigade. Fortunately for Ritchie, however, Brigadier H. R. Briggs, commander of the 7th Indian Brigade, divined Rommel's intentions at the last moment. Instead of ordering a withdrawal along the Via Balbia, which would have left his units open to a flank attack from the mountains, he ordered the brigade to break out to the south-east, across the face of the advancing XX Corps. The Italians, slow to react, let the majority of the brigade past, but over 1,000 Indian troops were caught and forced to surrender when the gap between the advancing Italians and Germans closed. Rommel captured Benghazi with minimal casualties, threw the 4th Indian Division into disorder, and took another major supply dump (the seven million cigarettes and twelve lorry-loads of rum captured heightened the morale of DAK considerably).

Godwin-Austen, infuriated by Ritchie's refusal to take his advice, resigned his command (although he was only a corps commander Godwin-Austen was the same rank as Ritchie, lieutenant-general, and had in fact been one rather longer than his commanding officer). Godwin-Austen was not the only senior officer casualty of Operation 'Theseus': General Gastone Gambara, Commander of XX Corps, was dismissed almost as soon as the campaign was over.

Rommel had neglected to tell his Italian superiors that he intended to launch a counter-offensive (indeed, he also failed to inform Berlin) but had taken Gambara into his confidence as he needed the tanks of the Ariete Armoured Division to be assured of success. Gambara had gone along with Rommel's plan without mentioning it to General Bastico.

Rommel was suspicious of the security of the Italian cipher system and did not tell Bastico of his plans because he was sure to signal Cavallero, his superior in Rome.

Bastico and Cavallero were furious with Rommel for attacking without formal permission, and as he was untouchable (in fact Hitler promoted Rommel to *Oberstgeneral* at the conclusion of 'Theseus') Gambara felt the full wrath of the Italian High Command, despite the fact he was clearly the most capable of the Italian field commanders. Petty jealousies, intercommand squabbling and incompetent leadership were rife in both Axis and Allied camps; Cavallero even went so far as to cancel all the forward movement orders of X and XXI Corps, leaving all the Italian infantry divisions at Mersa el Brega for the duration of 'Theseus'.

With the capture of Benghazi and the hasty retreat of the 4th Indian Division, Ritchie had no option but to relinquish the Cyrenaica bulge to the Axis and fall back on a prepared defensive position running south from Gazala, some 35 miles west of Tobruk. All the Allied troops were safely behind the new defence line by 4 February, the first German unit arriving to observe the Gazala position two days later. Rommel was slow to follow up, in part because of continued interference from Bastico and Cavallero, but mostly because a severe lack of fuel, even after using captured stocks, prevented him from sending units forward in anything other than dribs and drabs.

Left: AFPU (Army Film and Photographic Unit) cameramen usually worked in pairs on the battlefield. Here the stills photographer, half of the duo, takes a photograph of his compatriot who is busy filming a battle scene, 30 April 1942. (IWM E11067)

———————— CHAPTER SIX ————————

OPERATION 'VENEZIA'

It was to take Rommel nearly four months to gather together enough supplies, reinforcements and replacement vehicles to renew the offensive, with Panzerarmee Afrika (as Panzergruppe Afrika had been known since the end of 'Theseus'). In both March and April 1942 he had consulted with his superiors regarding a new assault to take Tobruk, as a first step of a strategy to capture Egypt.

Both the Italian and German High Commands were eager for any offensive to be delayed until after the conclusion of Operation 'Hercules', the planned invasion of Malta. The continual bombing of the island by the Axis air forces had reduced the ability of the Royal Navy and Royal Air Force to interfere with the shipment of supplies across the Mediterranean, and its capture would guarantee Rommel the logistical back-up he needed to undertake an invasion of Egypt.

German field intelligence was, however, worried that Ritchie was preparing an 8th Army offensive to begin in June or July. Rommel therefore sought and achieved permission to open his own offensive to pre-empt the Allies if at the end of May Malta had not fallen. Mussolini and Hitler agreed with Rommel but insisted that if this were the case Panzerarmee Afrika was to advance no farther forward than Tobruk. However, limita-

tions set by higher command had previously been blatantly ignored, and Rommel felt that they could be again if circumstances permitted. By mid-May it had become clear that the invasion of Malta was to be delayed, and Rommel decided it was time to strike.

Rommel's plan of attack for Operation 'Venezia' was relatively simple. Panzerarmee Afrika would be split into two main forces, Group Cruewell (the Italian X and XXI Corps, the German 15th Rifle Brigade and Kampfgruppe Kiehl, all commanded by General Ludwig Cruewell) and DAK, plus the Italian XX Corps, commanded by Rommel himself. A third force, consisting of the Bologna Infantry Division, the newly arrived

Littorio Armoured Division and assorted independent battalions (mostly combat-suspect Blackshirt formations) was held back as a reserve under the direct control of General Bastico.

The 15th Rifle Brigade, consisting of two regiments of infantry (four battalions), one of them the 361st Regiment borrowed from the 90th

Below: Rommel explains his plan for Operation 'Venezia'. From left to right are Colonel Westphal, Panzerarmee Afrika's Chief Operations Officer; Colonel von Mellenthin, Panzerarmee Afrika's Chief of Intelligence; Rommel himself; and General Nehring, Commander of the *Deutsches Afrika Korps* (DAK). (IWM HU5610)

Light Division, plus Kampfgruppe Kiehl (one anti-tank company, one anti-aircraft company, one squadron of PzKpfw IIs and two batteries of 88mm guns), were ordered to attack along the coast road towards Gazala. The appearance of German troops at the northern end of the Allied defence line would, it was hoped, pin significant numbers of infantry, and perhaps even tanks, in position. This would make the main thrust, at the extreme southern end of the line, that much easier. The Italian XXI Corps (Trento and Sabratha Divisions, commanded by General Enea Navarini) and X Corps (Pavia and Brescia Divisions, commanded by General Benvenuto Gioda) were to exert pressure on the northern and central sec-

Right: Rommel gives instructions on the deployment of the Afrika Korps to Nehring's Chief of Staff, Colonel Fritz Bayerlein, prior to the launching of Operation 'Venezia', May 1942. (IWM HU5628) Below: An Italian crew manning a German-built 37mm anti-tank gun watches a Stuka attack in progress on an Allied position. (IWM MH5850)

Right: A Semovente 75/18 self-propelled gun, Italy's most potent armoured vehicle during the desert campaign, seen here guarding a DAK headquarters group during the operations near Gazala, May/June 1942. (IWM HU32735)

tors of the defence line, again pinning the defending divisions in position. The Italian XX Corps (Ariete Armoured and Trieste Motorised Divisions, commanded by General Ettore Baldassare) formed the left flank of Rommel's force. They were to capture Bir Hacheim at the southern tip of the Allied defence line and act as a pivot on which DAK was to swing, round the bottom of the defences through the open desert and up into the Allied rear. DAK (General Walther Nehring) consisted of the 21st and 15th Panzer Divisions and the 90th Light Division, deployed in that order, north to south, at the southern end of the Axis line.

Facing them the 8th Army (Lieutenant-General Neil Ritchie) consisted of XIII Corps (1st and 2nd South African Divisions, and the 50th Infantry Division, commanded by Lieutenant-General 'Strafer' Gott) and XXX Corps (1st and 7th Armoured Divisions, commanded by Lieutenant-General Willoughby M. Norrie). The 5th Indian Division and the 1st Free French Brigade, also present, were controlled directly from Army Headquarters.

In terms of men and equipment the Allies had a large superiority over the Axis troops facing them; for example, an Allied infantry division contained nine infantry battalions compared to six in an Italian division, and each British armoured/tank brigade (of which there were five) contained three regiments/battalions against a total of twelve tank/self-propelled gun battalions (six of them Italian) fielded by the Axis. In total the British deployed 843 tanks in the Gazala battles, over a quarter of them new

American-built Grants with 75mm guns. The Axis fielded 333 German and 228 Italian tanks and self-propelled guns. They, too, had received new equipment. The Germans had 19 PzKpfw III Ausf Js armed with a high-velocity 50mm gun and having 20mm of extra frontal armour, and increasing numbers of Marder II tank destroyers armed with 76.2mm guns were replacing Marder I vehicles with 47mm guns in the two German Panzerjäger battalions.

The Italians also brought into service two battalions of new self-propelled guns, the Semovente 75/18. Despite the fact that its main armament, a low/medium velocity 75mm howitzer, could not be fired with the vehicle's hatches shut, tended to jam (Semovente crews always carried a

Below: A 75mm field gun manned by Free French Marines fires on an enemy position near Bir Hacheim, 4 April 1942. (IWM E10232)

long pole with which to fish out shell cases from the muzzle end!) and only had moderate armour penetration, it was still an improvement over the M13 tank.

It is interesting to note that at the outset of the offensive both Ritchie and Rommel thought that significant numbers of enemy troops were either deployed in places where they were not, or that units present on the battlefield were no longer in the enemy's order of battle. Consequently both generals felt that victory was going to be more easily achievable than it in fact was (Rommel estimated victory in five days!). This was due to a high standard of radio security on the part of the Allies, which meant that Rommel could not locate the 22nd Armoured Brigade, 32nd Army Tank Brigade, 201st Guards Brigade, 29th Indian Brigade or 3rd Indian Motor Brigade. Axis intelligence had also failed to discover that the extensive Allied minefields had spread as far south as Bir Hacheim, and that the oasis itself had been turned into a formidable fortress, defended by nearly 4,000 Free French troops. Allied intelligence was completely taken in by Rommel's pre-'Venezia' deception plan and the deployment of the 15th Rifle Brigade and Kampfgruppe Kiehl near the Via Balbia: on the opening day of the battle both Ritchie and Auchinleck expected the main enemy thrust to be made either along the coast road or through the centre of the Allied position.

To counter Rommel's suspected line of attack Ritchie deployed his forces as follows. XIII Corps defended the northern end of the Gazala Line, the 1st South African Division (1st, 2nd and 3rd South African Brigades) holding the sector from the coast to Alem Hamza, with the 32nd Army Tank Brigade (Matilda and Valentine tanks) in support. The 50th Infantry Division (69th, 150th and 151st Infantry Brigades) held the centre of the Allied line with the 1st Army Tank Brigade in support (again equipped with Matilda and Valentine tanks). The 2nd South African Division (4th and 6th South African Brigades) was held in reserve inside the Tobruk perimeter, except for small outposts of the 6th South African Brigade at Acroma and Point 209, north of Eluet et Tamar. The 9th Indian Brigade, temporarily attached to the South Africans, was also deployed in Tobruk, less one battalion which held the fortified El Adem Box south of the port. XXX Corps was deployed behind the main defence line. The 1st Armoured Division (2nd and 22nd Armoured Brigades, plus

Below: A two-man road-watching team of the LRDG (Long Range Desert Group) observes Axis traffic well behind enemy lines, 25 May 1942. These teams were a vital source of information about the movements of enemy formations, and their job was a highly dangerous and lonely one. Teams could expect to be behind enemy lines for several days at a time, unable to move at all throughout the blazing heat of the day in case they gave away their position. (IWM E12434)

the 201st Guards Brigade) was placed astride the Trigh Capuzzo and north of the Trigh el Abd. This was to counter the expected thrust through the centre of the Allied position. The 7th Armoured Division (4th Armoured Brigade and 7th Motor Brigade) was widely dispersed. The 4th Armoured Brigade was deployed alongside the 22nd Armoured Brigade, whilst the 7th Motor Brigade, less one battalion, had been pushed out in front of the defence line southwest of Bir Hacheim, just in case the Germans tried an outflanking manoeuvre. The detached battalion of the brigade was deployed in a defensive box at Retma. The 3rd Indian Motor Brigade held a defensive box to the south-east of Bir Hacheim, while the 29th Indian Brigade held Bir el Gubi and the 10th Indian Brigade was positioned as a reserve near

Gambut. Finally, the 1st Free French Brigade held a strong defensive position in and around Bir Hacheim itself.

During 26 May the mechanised and motorised forces of DAK and XX Corps moved to a concentration area east of Rotonda Segnali; fortunately, their movements were almost totally masked by a series of sandstorms which blew up across the desert. At the same time Group Cruewell advanced against the Gazala Line, supported by a heavy and prolonged artillery bombardment. Operation 'Venezia' had begun.

After nightfall Rommel placed himself in the van of the Afrika Korps, and, taking advantage of a full moon, he led them south towards the southern end of the Gazala Defence Line. The immense column of several thousand vehicles stopped to refuel

Above: Men of the Natal Mounted Rifles come under heavy mortar fire in their fox-hole positions, 22 May 1942. (IWM E12296)

south-east of Bir Hacheim and then waited for dawn when the attack proper was to begin.

At the time Rommel was sure the southward move had not been spotted, but in fact armoured cars of the 4th South African Armoured Car Regiment had been carefully monitoring the advance for several miles, and detailed reports were sent back to both the 7th Motor Brigade and the 7th Armoured Division Headquarters. Fortunately for DAK, General Messervy, now in command of the 7th Armoured Division, failed to pass any warning on to Corps or Army Command, although the 7th Motor Brigade were told to be ready to fall back

in the face of this markedly superior force. This meant that units in the path of the Axis outflanking manoeuvre not belonging to the 7th Armoured Division (such as the 3rd Indian Motor Brigade) were taken completely by surprise the next morning.

The attack began well, with the Ariete Armoured Division overwhelming the box defended by the 3rd Indian Motor Brigade, and the 90th Light Division, with the 3rd and 33rd Reconnaissance Battalions in support, sweeping over the smaller Retma Box, held by a battalion of the 7th Motor Brigade. The 15th Panzer Division, in the centre of the advance, caught the 4th Armoured Brigade while it was still deploying for battle. After heavy fighting the British were driven from the field, the 8th Hussars being destroyed as a fighting unit and the 3rd RTR losing 16 of its brand new Grant tanks. The disasters continued, with the 7th Armoured Division Headquarters captured intact on the move (Messervy managed to escape the next day) by the 8th Panzer Regiment. The famed 7th Armoured Division was fleeing for the comparative safety of El Adem (4th Armoured Brigade) and Bir el Gubi (7th Motor Brigade) within four hours of its armour having been brought to contact. The 90th Light Division followed in hot pursuit.

The 1st Armoured Division fared little better. At 8.45 a.m. the 22nd Armoured Brigade (3rd and 4th County of London Yeomanry, 2nd Royal

Left, upper: SdKfz 222 armoured cars of a DAK reconnaissance battalion probe forward during Operation 'Venezia'. (IWM HU5626)
Left, lower: A DAK infantryman checks his watch as zero hour approaches. (IWM HU5624)
Right, upper: PzKpfw IV tanks of the 5th Panzer Regiment in action. (IWM GER619)
Right, lower: Operation 'Venezia': the opening phase, 27 May 1942.

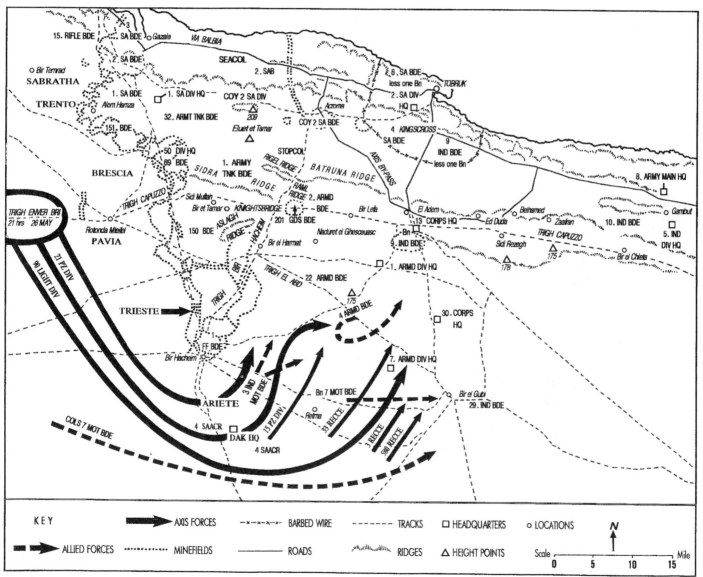

Left: DAK panzers on the move along a desert track during Operation 'Venezia'. (IWM HU40328)

Below: A burning truck is all that remains of an Axis supply column intercepted by a Free French mechanised patrol; the remainder of the column fled the scene as soon as the firing started, 4 April 1942. Hit-and-run raids such as this from Bir Hacheim and other desert outposts were to cause Rommel severe problems during the Gazala battles. (IWM E10203)

Gloucestershire Hussars) was ordered to move south to engage the enemy. The 15th Panzer Division, this time with the tanks of the 21st Panzer Division in support, attacked the still deploying British brigade from both flanks, while an anti-tank gun screen held the centre of the German position. Within an hour the 22nd Armoured Brigade was in full retreat.

Rommel ordered Nehring to press on, sure that victory was close. At midday, whilst DAK were trying to force a crossing of the Trigh Capuzzo, they were attacked yet again by British tanks, this time by Matildas of the 1st Army Tank Brigade and Grants and Crusaders from the 2nd Armoured Brigade. Neither brigade coordinated its attack with the other, with the inevitable consequence that

they were defeated piecemeal and driven off.

However, over eight hours of continuous combat against four successive British armoured brigades had taken its toll on the 15th and 21st Panzer Divisions and Rommel, at least on one occasion, considered a withdrawal. By mid-afternoon, low on fuel and ammunition, exhausted and with heavy casualties sustained in the extremely fierce close-range fighting, DAK came to a halt astride the Trigh Capuzzo. If only the two British armoured divisions, or even the brigades within a division, had been able coordinate their attacks on Rommel's force, victory would probably have gone to the Allies.

By the end of the first day's fighting DAK had lost over one-third of its complement of panzers, but it was

positioned deep in the Allied rear ready to exploit its position. The 15th and 21st Panzer Divisions leaguered for the night in 'hedgehog' formation (that is, surrounded by an anti-tank gun and infantry screen) between the Rigel Ridge and Bir Lefa. The Ariete Division, having failed to take Bir

Below: A British patrol takes prisoner two Germans using an Italian supply truck, south of Bir Hacheim, 2 June 1942. The Germans had mistaken the British patrol's vehicles as their own (a common occurrence in the desert due both to the heat haze and to the fact that the Axis used hundreds of captured Allied vehicles) and were consequently taken without a fight. At this time the British patrol estimated that they were some 12 miles behind the enemy lines. (IWM E12810)

Right: An 88mm FlaK being used in a ground role against British armour during the Gazala battles, late May/early June 1942. Note the large number of kill rings on the guns barrel. (IWM HU70984)

Hacheim, leaguered near Bir el Harmat (the Trieste Division was still struggling to force a passage through the extensive minefields to the north of the Free French position). The 90th Light Division, after having reached the El Adem crossroads, had been counter-attacked by the 4th Armoured Brigade and had been forced to 'hedgehog' south of El Adem.

Despite DAK's battlefield victories Rommel was acutely aware of how tenuous his position was. In effect the 1st Free French Brigade at Bir Hacheim and the 29th Indian and 7th Motor Brigades at Bir el Gubi were now behind his front line. These fortified positions could and would act as bases from which Allied motorised and armoured car units could cut across his lines of communication, starving his forward units of fuel and ammunition. If on 28 May Ritchie had concentrated the remaining ar-

mour of the 22nd and 2nd Armoured Brigades, along with the battered 1st Army Tank Brigade and the as yet uncommitted 32nd Army Tank Brigade, which were all in the immediate vicinity of the 15th and 21st Panzer Divisions, there is no doubt that an attack would have overwhelmed the Axis positions. Instead the 22nd Armoured Brigade spent the day 'observing' the 15th Panzer Division on Rigel Ridge; the 1st Army Tank Bri-

gade and the 2nd Armoured Brigade launched yet more uncoordinated attacks, this time against the Ariete Armoured Division; and the 32nd Army Tank Brigade did nothing at all. The 4th Armoured Brigade, instead of moving to link up with other Allied units, spent the entire day at-

Below: Italian infantry wait to move forward against a British defensive position. (IWM MH5825)

tacking the 90th Light Division south of El Adem. The 90th Light, without any panzers but with a plentiful supply of anti-tank guns, were quite happy for the British tanks to throw themselves at their defensive position. It seems that the British armoured commanders had learnt little or nothing about inter-unit coordination, or the pointlessness of charging headlong at panzer or anti-tank gun screens, from the disasters of Operation 'Crusader'.

Rommel was mightily relieved that the British did not press home a mass tank attack against DAK. The Allies did not realise it, but by mid-morning on 28 May the 15th Panzer Division was completely out of fuel and

was stranded on Rigel Ridge. The 21st Panzer Division pressed on to the north, capturing Point 209 from a battalion of the 6th South African Brigade and manoeuvring into position on the escarpment overlooking the Via Balbia. The Axis had now cut or were in a position to fire upon every road or track that ran to the Gazala Line. Rommel could smell victory just around the corner. But his plans were to be dashed by the almost total lack of supplies getting through to DAK and XX Corps. An urgent request was sent out to Group Cruewell for a set-piece assault to be made on the Gazala Line, so that a gap could be created through which supplies could be funnelled. Cruewell

was not sure that such an attack would succeed, especially with the relatively low-grade Italian infantry he had under his command. Nevertheless he ordered the Sabratha Division to prepare an attack against the 1st South African Brigade for the next day.

In the meantime Rommel took a personal interest in DAK's logistics problems and set out at dawn on 29 May to find a route through which supply columns could pass relatively unmolested. At the same time the Sabratha Division's attack went in against Alem Hamza, but it was

Below: Operation 'Venezia': day two, 28 May 1942.

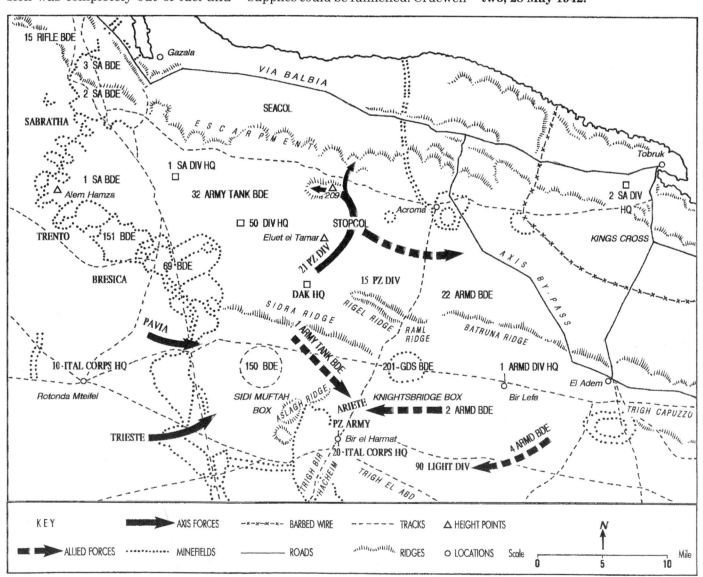

Above: Looking from Knightsbridge and the Guards' defensive box towards The Cauldron, 1 June 1942. (IWM E12690)
Below: The crew of a DAK SdKfz 250 half-track observe an engagement on the horizon, May/ June 1942. (IWM HU32631)

moured car patrols and managed to link up with the lead units of the Trieste Division south of the Sidi Muftah Box. By midday he was back at DAK Headquarters with a large supply column, enough to get the 15th Panzer Division moving again— and only just in time.

That afternoon the 2nd Armoured Brigade launched a fierce attack westwards from Knightsbridge in an attempt to drive a wedge between the Ariete Armoured Division, south of the Trigh Capuzzo, and DAK to the north. However, with the intervention of tanks from the 8th Panzer Regiment the attack was turned back. Late in the afternoon the 22nd Armoured Brigade launched its own attack along the same axis, but this, too, was rebuffed. Once again there had been a lamentable lack of coordination and communication between the two armoured brigades of the 1st Armoured Division. The 4th Armoured Brigade remained in reserve for most of the day, moving up into contact with the 90th Light Division towards dusk.

In spite of considerable casualties for the Panzer divisions, the 90th Light and the Ariete, the day ended to Rommel's advantage. All four divisions were now in close contact, gathered around the Trigh Capuzzo–Trigh Bir Hacheim crossroads. However, the acute lack of supplies, particularly fuel and ammunition, getting through to DAK forced a re-evaluation of the situation on Rommel. The supply column that had got through had barely met the needs of the 15th and 21st Panzer Divisions for one day. The intended supply route around the southern tip of the Gazala Line was clearly impracticable, at least until such time as the garrison at Bir Hacheim had been eliminated. Reluctantly Rommel gave the order for DAK and the Ariete to fall back to the south-west on the gap created in the British

beaten back by heavy artillery and infantry fire, the division losing over 400 men (many of them taken prisoner) in the assault.

Rommel, in grave personal danger, drove south-east through a veritable swarm of Allied motorised and ar-

minefield by the Trieste Division. The move was to begin the next day.

Group Cruewell had also suffered a major blow on the 29th. Cruewell himself had been shot down and captured whilst he was flying between his headquarters and that of the Italian X Corps. Fortunately Field Marshal Kesselring arrived the same day to assess the progress of the offensive and he was persuaded to take command until a suitable replacement could be found. Although Group Cruewell (as it continued to be known) had failed to penetrate the northern end of the Gazala Line, the Pavia Division of X Corps had managed to open a breach in the centre of the Allied position. The 50th Infantry Division was stretched out on too wide a front and its 150th Infantry Brigade had been forced to adopt an all-round defensive posture in the Sidi Muftah Box, owing to the proximity of large numbers of enemy tanks to the brigade's rear. This had left sections of the Gazala Line unguarded and a lane through the minefields had been made near the Trigh Capuzzo.

Further south the Trieste Division had also had success creating a breach in the minefields. A 15-mile gap in the Allied line had been left unmanned between the 150th Infantry Brigade and the 1st Free French

Right, upper: General Ludwig Cruewell eats a hearty lunch at an accommodating officers' mess soon after his capture, 29 May 1942. (IWM E12659)
Right, lower: An 88mm dual-purpose gun in a desert emplacement. This weapon gave Rommel a tremendous advantage in anti-tank capability over the Allies. This particular piece has 39 visible 'kill' rings (no doubt several more are obscured by the crewman standing in front of the barrel), indicating a fearful toll in British tanks from this one gun alone. (IWM STT1344)

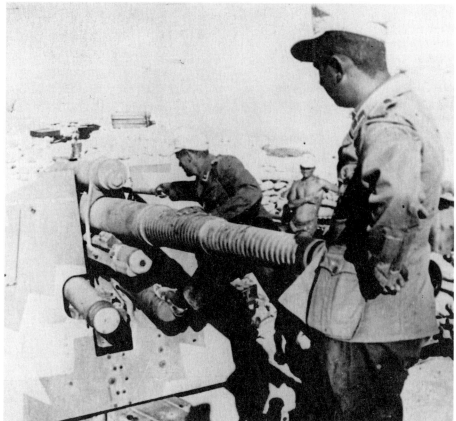

Above: The commander of a Stuart light tank surveys the desert for signs of the enemy, next to the smoking hull of a destroyed German PzKpfw III, 1 June 1942. (IWM E12670)

Brigade at Bir Hacheim. Minefields in themselves do not stop attackers, they just slow them down; it is troops covering the minefields with fire that stop enemy breakthroughs. This elementary tactical concept had been ignored by the British and, as a consequence, by 30 May several lanes had been cleared through the Gazala Line north of Bir Hacheim. These gaps made by the Italians were to be of great value to Rommel when he withdrew to the Sidi Muftah area on that day. In the afternoon Rommel

himself drove through one of the gaps in the Gazala Line to consult with Kesselring on what would be the most appropriate next step in Operation 'Venezia'.

While this meeting took place DAK and the Ariete Division withdrew to a position bounded by the Sidra Ridge to the north, the Aslagh Ridge to the east and British-laid minefields to the south. Gaps in the minefields to the west ensured that supplies were now reaching the armoured formations. This area became known as 'The Cauldron' and was to see the fiercest fighting of the Gazala battle. Trapped right in the centre of The Cauldron was the 150th Infantry Brigade, in its defensive box at Sidi Muftah. The brigade did its

best to disrupt the flow of supplies through the minefields by continually shelling the breaches, and Rommel was concerned that if a concerted attack were made by British armour upon either the Sidra or the Aslagh Ridges they would be able to link up with the Sidi Muftah Box and the Axis position behind the Gazala Line would become untenable.

He need not have worried. The British armoured brigades had lost heart at the continual drubbings handed out by Rommel's armour, and although the 2nd and 22nd Armoured Brigades did try a half-hearted attack they called it off as soon as they ran into a battery of 88mm guns blocking their path. It is interesting to note that no German tanks were present during this engagement and that, if the armoured brigades had called upon artillery support to suppress the anti-tank guns with high-explosive fire, the advance would have been able to resume after only a little delay. However, the dreaded 88s spread a fear far out of proportion to their numbers and the Axis were left to consolidate The Cauldron position in peace; in fact the Axis forces east of the Gazala Line were left alone by British armour for nearly five days, while they received reinforcements and replacement tanks.

By the end of 30 May the 21st Panzer Division (less the 5th Panzer Regiment, which was detailed to cover the valley between the two ridges) was deployed along the Sidra Ridge, in front of which German engineers hurriedly began to sow mines, the Ariete Armoured Division occupied the Aslagh Ridge and the 90th Light and Trieste Divisions encircled the Sidi Muftah Box in case the Allies tried to make a thrust through their own minefields.

The next day the attack began on the Sidi Muftah Box. Totally surrounded, the infantry of the 4th and 5th Battalions Green Howards and the 4th Battalion East Yorkshire Regiment, along with the 25pdrs of the 72nd Field Regiment Royal Artillery and Matildas from the 44th RTR, tried desperately to hold off the attacking enemy, who outnumbered them by at least three to one.

It looked at one point as though they might succeed, the infantry of the 288th Panzer Grenadier Regiment getting bogged down in the lodgement they had managed to make in the perimeter defences. Rommel, realising that the assault might well stall if the attackers did not regain their impetus, again placed himself in immense danger. Taking command of the lead company of the panzer grenadiers, he personally led the charge that broke through into the interior of the Sidi Muftah Box.

Once the perimeter of the British defences had been breached the final outcome of the battle was no longer in doubt. Although sections of the box continued to resist until 1 June, the battle for Sidi Muftah had been won. The next day the remaining 3,000 British troops in the box surrendered. For the two days it took fully to consolidate the interior of The Cauldron position the 8th Army did absolutely nothing to help the defenders of Sidi Muftah. The only support received by the 150th Brigade, despite the fighting being within corps artillery range, was from the RAF, who sporadically bombed the Axis positions.

The elimination of the 150th Infantry Brigade greatly eased Rommel's position, and on 2 June he sent the 90th Light and Trieste Divisions south to attack Bir Hacheim. More cautious, now that his original plan had failed, he had decided methodically to clean up the pockets of resistance to his rear before contemplating another major assault. Meanwhile the majority of his mechanised force waited in their Cauldron positions, ready for the inevitable Allied counter-attack.

Below: A British infantryman furiously digs in at a newly occupied desert position while his comrade gives cover with a Bren gun, 1 June 1942. (IWM E12665)

with anti-tank guns and dug-in infantry with no infantry support at all, and only two batteries of medium artillery for indirect fire support (despite the fact that at least another two regiments of medium artillery were readily available). The 10th Indian Brigade was detailed to undertake a night attack on the Aslagh Ridge and open a breach in the defensive position of the Ariete Division, through which the 22nd Armoured Brigade would pass into the interior of The Cauldron. The 9th Indian Brigade were to follow in the wake of the armour and consolidate the ground won by the 10th Indian Brigade. What at first glance appeared to be a bold first attempt to use infantry and tanks in a coordinated manner was on closer examination yet another piecemeal attack, one brigade committed after the other, allowing the Italian defenders to outnumber the attackers at every stage of the assault. To make matters worse, the command system adopted to oversee the attack broke down almost immediately. XIII Corps (Gott) was placed in charge of the attack on Sidra Ridge, whilst XXX Corps (Norrie) oversaw the assault on Aslagh Ridge. At no time during the attack did the two corps commanders cooperate or communicate. The Aslagh Ridge assault was further complicated by the fact that the 5th Indian Division Headquarters was placed in charge whilst the 10th Indian Brigade carried out its night attack; control of the operation was then transferred to the 7th Armoured Division when the 22nd Armoured Brigade moved forward, with command reverting to 5th Indian Division when the 9th Indian Brigade was committed.

The assault, when it came, was badly planned and badly carried out, despite the fact that Ritchie and his corps commanders had taken nearly five days to organise the operation. It was finally decided to mount a two-pronged attack on the Axis position. The 32nd Army Tank Brigade would assault the Sidra Ridge, while the 9th and 10th Indian Brigades, plus the 22nd Armoured Brigade, attacked the Aslagh Ridge. Thus Ritchie was committing to the offensive about one-half of the combat troops he had available in the area (for example, both the 2nd and 4th Armoured Brigades sat out the battle nearby). This scandalous under-use of resources was exacerbated by the terrible way in which the troops committed were employed and by the ponderous and over-complicated command structure which was devised to administer the operation.

The 32nd Army Tank Brigade was ordered to attack a ridge line bristling

Right: A Grant tank of the 22nd Armoured Brigade moves forward during the fighting in The Cauldron area, June 1942. The vehicle in the distance is in fact a dummy Grant tank of 101 RTR, a fictitious unit created to mislead Rommel as to the numbers of British tanks in the field. (IWM HU68710)

This command structure was nonsensical. What was needed was for control of the overall operation to be assigned to one of the two corps commanders, who would then be allowed to draw upon all the available assets of the 8th Army, regardless of which formation they belonged to. This 'mix and match' system was used superbly by the Germans, whose *ad hoc* Kampfgruppen of units drawn from every available formation (including Italian units) outmanoeuvred and outfought the Allies time after time.

The failure to provide the 32nd Army Tank Brigade with adequate artillery support—we will ignore the utter failure to allocate the brigade any infantry support—was a prime example of the rigid inflexibility of the Allied organisational system. Two-thirds of XIII Corps' medium artillery had been assigned to the 1st South African Division prior to the launching of 'Venezia'. It seems that Gott was unable or unwilling to reassign these batteries to support the attack on Sidra Ridge, despite having four days to organise their change of role and the fact that pressure on the South Africans was decreasing, not increasing. Allied (particularly British) senior commanders viewed the units under their control as theirs and no one else's. Consequently, when battlefield tasks arose that needed inter-formation cooperation, they either did not get done or ponderous and unworkable command structures had to evolve to enable all the relevant commanders to keep their fingers in their pies.

This tactical and strategic inflexibility explains why British armoured brigades attacked Axis mechanised formations time after time without adequate infantry support. Their commanders' reasoning went thus. If a particular battlefield task had needed infantry support, then an infantry brigade would have been assigned to carry out the task. It was the job of British tanks to engage and destroy enemy armour; panzer divisions ought then to be left to the 'experts', the armoured brigades. Com-

Left: The driver and co-driver of a British supply truck hug the ground under artillery fire. Their movement across the open desert had attracted the attention of an Axis observer and they were forced to flee their vehicle until the bombardment ended, 4 June 1942. (IWM E12870)

bined-arms cooperation was a thing of theory for most British field commanders, and would remain so until well into 1943.

Because of this blinkered attitude Operation 'Aberdeen', as Ritchie dubbed the attack on The Cauldron, was a complete disaster. Auchinleck had stressed to Ritchie the vital importance of close cooperation between infantry and tanks and the need for a thorough reconnaissance of the enemy's positions. As we have already seen, Ritchie totally ignored his superior's advice, stating that there had been 'plenty of time for recce' and that his commanders were confident, 'full of beans and happy'. This was far

from the truth. The British had carried out little in the way of forward reconnaissance. For example, they did not know that German engineers had sown minefields in front of the Sidra Ridge, nor did they spot the lanes created in the British minefields to the south of the Aslagh Ridge (these were made on the express orders of Rommel to allow German tank recovery teams to retrieve damaged vehicles in the Bir el Harmat area).

The Allied commanders were not at all happy with Ritchie's plan of attack. Brigadier Fletcher, in command of the 9th Indian Brigade, was particularly scathing of its over-optimistic tone. The lack of reconnaissance was highlighted further when the attack's preliminary artillery bombardment landed, for the most part, on empty desert, the Ariete Division having abandoned the positions shelled a few days previously to fall back to a new defence line several hundred yards further west.

Nevertheless the assault went in as planned at dawn on 5 June. After very heavy fighting, in which both sides took large numbers of casualties, the 10th Indian Brigade was able to establish itself on Aslagh Ridge, the Italian infantry falling back towards their corps headquarters. The 22nd Armoured Brigade and the 9th Indian Brigade then pushed on into The Cauldron's interior.

This is where the attack broke down. German and Italian tanks counter-attacked and forced the 22nd Armoured Brigade to retreat east of Bir et Tamar. The 9th Indian Brigade was then left alone to face the Axis armour and the now re-advancing Italian infantry. Without tank support they too were forced to retreat through the gap between the Sidra and Aslagh Ridges. Once again Axis forces had attacked Allied formations in turn and had defeated them piecemeal. At no time during the battle

Below: 25pdr field guns pound enemy positions in preparation for a night attack, the one form of desert warfare at which the Allies were consistently better throughout the campaign, 2 June 1942. (IWM E12790)

was any attempt made for Indian infantry to support British armour or vice versa. Brigadier Fletcher, in charge of the Indian formation, later stated, 'There seems to have been a complete misunderstanding between 22nd Armoured Brigade and 9th Indian Brigade as to the capabilities and tasks of the two brigades.'

Meanwhile the 32nd Army Tank Brigade assaulted Sidra Ridge. The attack was doomed from the start and the brigade's Matildas failed even to reach the German front line. The slow-moving tanks provided excellent targets for the 21st Panzer Division's

Right: Wounded members of a British anti-tank gun battery receive medical attention after seeing off a panzer attack near Knightsbridge, 4 June 1942. (IWM E12853)
Below: A Grant tank passes a PzKpfw I it had earlier destroyed in a desert encounter, 6 June 1942. (IWM E12920)

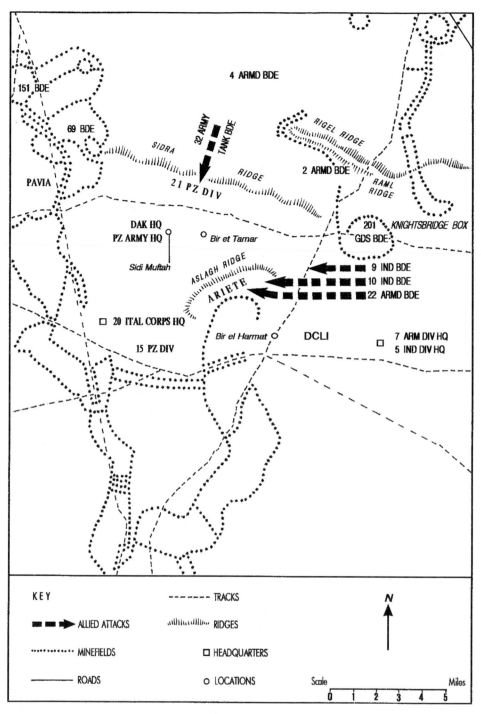

KEY

------- TRACKS

▪▪▪▶ ALLIED ATTACKS

⠀⠀⠀⠀⠀⠀ RIDGES

·········· MINEFIELDS

☐ HEADQUARTERS

―― ROADS

○ LOCATIONS

Scale

N

0 1 2 3 4 5 Miles

Left: Operation 'Aberdeen': the attack on The Cauldron, 5 June 1942.

wards Bir el Harmat. The left flank of the British line was held by the 1st Battalion Duke of Cornwall's Light Infantry, recently arrived in North Africa from Baghdad and with no desert combat experience. Without a single tank or anti-tank gun they stood absolutely no chance of holding back the tidal wave of German armour and were destroyed utterly.

The next victims of the southern panzer thrust were the combined headquarters of Generals Messervy and Briggs (7th Armoured Division and 5th Indian Division), which were overrun with ease. Rommel then ordered the attack to swing north towards Knightsbridge, along the Trigh Bir Hacheim. Meanwhile the Italian and German attack north of the Aslagh Ridge had thrown back the demoralised 9th Indian Brigade and 22nd Armoured Brigade with considerable losses and in some confusion. The two Axis thrusts linked up at nightfall south-east of the Knightsbridge Box.

The 10th Indian Brigade, four regiments of field artillery and the 22nd Armoured Brigade's support units were now trapped on or behind the Aslagh Ridge. They could have been saved had the 2nd, 4th and 22nd Armoured Brigades mounted a coordinated counter-attack the next day, but no such assault materialised. Instead the British armour spent 6 June moving and counter-moving in response to contradictory orders from their brigade, division and corps headquarters. Ritchie had lost his grip—tenuous from the very start— on the Allied field formations. Morale was low among the senior British officers, brigadiers no longer trusted their divisional commanders, and they in turn ignored the orders of their corps commanders. Everyone

anti-tank gunners, and they become sitting ducks when the advance blundered into the German minefields and came to a halt. Fifty of the 70 attacking tanks were destroyed, the survivors retreating as fast as they could back out of range.

By midday it was clear that the attack had failed and that the Allies were off-balance. Rommel decided to counter-attack. The tanks of the

Ariete Armoured Division and 21st Panzer Division, along with Ariete's motorised infantry, struck east from Bir et Tamar, between the two ridge lines. The remainder of the Ariete Division moved up to contain the 10th Indian Brigade on the Aslagh Ridge. The 15th Panzer Division, with Rommel in the van of the attack, struck east through the minefield gaps south of the Aslagh Ridge, to-

ignored Ritchie. As a consequence, after a day of heavy fighting on Aslagh Ridge, the 10th Indian Brigade and its associated units were forced to surrender. Rommel captured another 3,100 infantry, 96 field guns and 37 anti-tank guns as a direct result of the Allies' inability to react quickly or decisively. Operation 'Aberdeen' had seen the 10th Indian Brigade wiped out, the 9th Indian Brigade badly mauled and over 100 tanks (32nd Army Tank Brigade and 22nd Armoured Brigade) lost. Confidence in the Allied camp was at an all-time low.

Instead of pushing on immediately into the Allied rear Rommel decided to eliminate the troublesome fortress of Bir Hacheim first. This would prevent any repeat of earlier events, when DAK supply columns had been severely harassed by light forces operating in the Axis rear. A strong detachment of the 15th Panzer Division was therefore moved south to augment the infantry of the Trieste and 90th Light Divisions, who were

making slow progress in the face of very determined French resistance. By 9 June the Germans had managed to capture Point 186, a hillock overlooking the main French position, and in the night of 10/11 June the French garrison felt compelled to break out. This they did expertly, managing to withdraw with most of

Above: The crew of a German anti-tank gun (possibly a captured Russian 76mm piece) relax after knocking out a probing British tank, May/June 1942. (IWM MH5862)
Below: Foreign Legionnaires of the 1st Free French Brigade at Bir Hacheim rush an enemy strongpoint, June 1942. (IWM E13313)

their force intact. The Free French stand at Bir Hacheim had tied up two and a half Axis divisions and had prevented a decisive panzer thrust into the Allied rear, not once but twice.

In spite of all these victories Rommel was still at a disadvantage numerically on the Gazala battlefield. Even at this late stage in the battle Ritchie still disposed 250 cruiser and 80 infantry tanks, compared to 160 German and 70 Italian tanks available to the Axis. Rommel still had a large and well dug-in Allied force to deal with. A line of defensive boxes, protected by minefields, had been built up to the north of The Cauldron (manned mostly by infantry of the 6th South African Brigade), the 201st Guards Brigade was firmly ensconced in the Knightsbridge Box, the 29th Indian Brigade held a box south of El Adem and the 7th Motorised Brigade defended the old Italian fortifications at Bir el Gubi. Behind them the 2nd South African Division and 11th Indian Brigade held Tobruk, while the 20th and 21st Indian Brigades and the 2nd Free French Brigade held the sector Sidi Rezegh–Gambut. The 1st South African Division and 50th Infantry Division still held the Gazala Line, north of The Cauldron, holding the Italian XXI Corps and the German 15th Rifle Brigade at bay.

To bring about the final collapse of the 8th Army Rommel reverted to a modified model of the original 'Venezia' plan. While the 21st Panzer Division demonstrated against

Left, upper: A bayonet charge by 8th Army infantry past a dead German towards an enemy strongpoint, 6 June 1942. (IWM E12922)
Left, lower: A PzKpfw IV of the 15th Panzer Division moves past an abandoned Bren Carrier, Bir Hacheim, early June 1942. (IWM HU70996)

the defences to the north of The Cauldron (in the hope that British armour would be dragged in this direction), the 15th Panzer Division, with the 90th Light Division on its right flank and the Trieste Division on its left flank, was ordered to sweep towards El Adem. Once captured, this was to provide a springboard from which an advance to the coast east of Tobruk would be made, cutting off the Allied field army and, it was hoped, capturing the port in a surprise attack. The Ariete Armoured Division was ordered to hold the area around Bir el Harmat, thus providing a link between the 21st Panzer Division and the outflanking attack and forming the pivot on which the sweeping manoeuvre would be made.

The new advance began in the afternoon of 11 June. By the time darkness fell the 15th Panzer Division had reached Naduret el Ghesceuasc, about 12 miles south-east of its objective. The 90th Light Division had advanced to a position due south of the 29th Indian Brigade's box, while the Trieste Division lagged some way behind south-west of Bir el Harmat. Thus the attacking force was spread over a front of nearly 20 miles, and was very vulnerable to a concerted Allied counter-attack. In particular,

Right, upper: Two Free French infantrymen make their way to the rear after evacuating Bir Hacheim, 11 June 1942. From their mode of dress it can be deduced that they have been in continuous action for a long time—no time for spit and polish here! (IWM E13397)
Right, lower: Both sides attempted to recover broken-down tanks from the battlefield (the Germans were better at it than the British) to bolster their ever-flagging armoured resources. Here a British tank recovery team dives for cover after its attempts to haul away a disabled Crusader attracted the attention of Axis artillery, 8 June 1942. (IWM E13083)

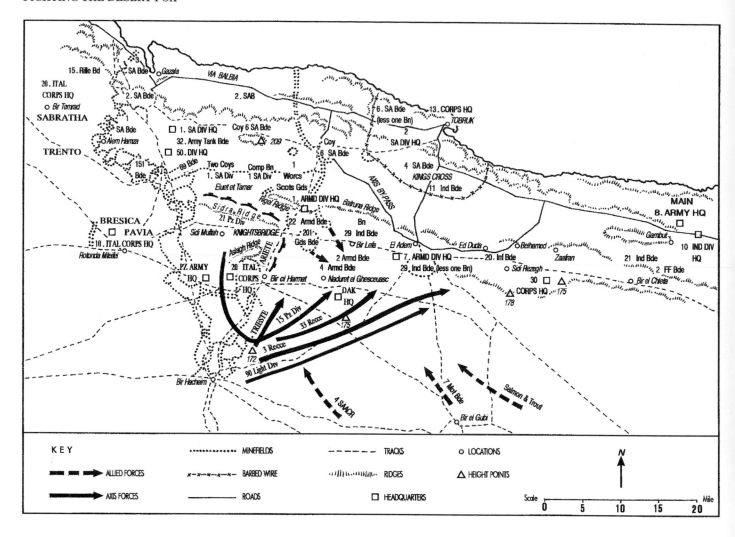

the 90th Light Division, now down to less than 2,000 effectives, was positioned between the 29th Indian Brigade south of El Adem and the 7th Motorised Brigade at Bir el Gubi. A double envelopment could have spelt disaster for Rommel.

Fortunately no such move was contemplated by Ritchie. A counter-attack was organised, but it was to be made by the 2nd and 4th Armoured Brigades against the 15th Panzer Division, the British commander-in-chief strangely choosing to assault the strongest point of Rommel's advance with two battered brigades rather than the weakest point in his line with two fresh ones. To make matters even worse, poor wireless security meant that Rommel knew of the impending attack and was able to take effective counter-measures:

the 15th Panzer Division was ordered to halt, deploy its anti-tank guns and make ready for a tank assault, while the 21st Panzer Division was ordered to disengage, move south-east and hit the British armour in the rear.

The Allied attack of 12 June was slow to develop, mainly due to the arguments raging between the British field commanders. Messervy (Commander, 7th Armoured Division) saw the futility of yet another frontal attack on German armour and wanted to pull his division off to Bir el Gubi, where it could reunite with the 7th Motorised Brigade and operate against the Axis flank. His two armoured brigade commanders had apparently learned nothing from their desert combat experience and they fully concurred with Ritchie's ridiculous frontal assault idea. To

Above: Operation 'Venezia': the offensive resumes, 11 June 1942. Right, upper: A wounded soldier is brought in to a Forward Dressing Station, 12 June 1942; in the background a medical officer tends to an earlier arrival. (IWM E13328) Right, lower: Here a column of RAMC (Royal Army Medical Corps) ambulances has just been strafed from the air by Axis fighters. The wounded driver of the smoking vehicle just out of frame is helped back to another ambulance from the column, 12 June 1942. (IWM E13334)

press home his argument Messervy drove off to speak to Ritchie in person but was nearly captured by a patrol of the 90th Light Division, probing its way northwards around the El Adem Box. His delay in the desert severely disrupted the British

plan of attack, postponing it for several hours, and Messervy did not get his way.

Fearing that the British attack was not going to materialise, General Nehring ordered the 15th Panzer Division to advance north-west, away from its El Adem objective but towards the last known position of the enemy's armour. It soon ran into the tentatively advancing British tanks and a fierce battle ensued. Things were fairly even until the 21st Panzer Division crashed into the flank of the 4th Armoured Brigade, then the battle swung decisively in favour of the Germans. The 22nd Armoured Brigade, responding to radioed calls for help from the engaged British armour, was effectively seen off by a 21st Panzer Division anti-tank gun screen, losing most of its remaining tanks in the process.

Under the converging pressure of the two panzer divisions, the 2nd and 4th Armoured Brigades gave way. The retreat of the 4th Armoured Brigade rapidly turned into a headlong rout over the Raml Ridge, north of the Knightsbridge position. The 2nd Armoured Brigade, along with the few surviving tanks of the 22nd Armoured Brigade, fell back on the Guards' positions in the Knightsbridge Box. During the day's fighting the British had lost over 120 tanks, and their armoured brigades had finally ceased to exist as viable fighting formations.

On 13 June Rommel decided to take advantage of the catastrophe that had befallen the British armour and shifted the axis of the German advance away from El Adem towards Rigel Ridge, Point 209 and Eluet et Tamar. The thrust north would now aim to reach the sea west of Tobruk. This would still trap two Allied divisions, and the distance to advance was much shorter, giving Rommel a much greater chance of success. It also allowed the Axis formations to

re-concentrate. The fleeting chance the Allies had of hitting the German formations spread out over the desert had now gone.

With the two panzer formations in the van the Axis advance rolled on towards the sea. During the afternoon of 13 June the Germans overran a defensive position on Rigel Ridge held by the Scots Guards and South African anti-tank guns, weak relieving attacks by British armour being beaten off. The Axis were now in possession of a ridge line dominating the immediate area. The Knightsbridge Box was now isolated behind the German lines, and during the night of 13/14 June most of its defenders (201st Guards Brigade) slipped away to the north-east.

In the morning of 14 June Ritchie finally accepted that the battle was lost and ordered the 1st South African and 50th Infantry Divisions to pull back as fast as they could along the coast road before they were cut off. At the same time Rommel exhorted his men onward for one final push to the sea which would seal decisive victory. However, the German formations were exhausted by over two weeks of continuous combat, and although they tried to advance as quickly as possible the majority of the

Above: The crew of a DAK SdKfz 250 half-track keep a close eye on enemy movements on the horizon, May/June 1942. (IWM HU32629) Right: Operation 'Venezia': the pursuit, 15 June 1942.

1st South African Division were able to escape. They were magnificently aided by a staunch rearguard defence by the 1st Battalion Worcestershire Regiment, a composite South African infantry battalion and a few British tanks, at Eluet et Tamar, which held up the German advance for several vital hours.

Unfortunately for Rommel, many of the men of the 50th Infantry Division were also able to get away, although they had to abandon all their heavy equipment and guns. In a desperate break-out attempt they burst through the lines of the Pavia Division and drove south as fast as they could, around the tip of the Gazala Line at Bir Hacheim and back to safety via Bir el Gubi. The Italian infantry divisions, totally lacking in motorised transport, could do nothing to stop them once the breach in their line had been made. Nevertheless, Rommel had won a major victory against the odds, and the bulk of the 8th Army was now in full retreat towards the frontier.

The next major task he faced was the elimination of the remaining strongpoints around Tobruk and the capture of the port itself. Both Auchinleck and Rommel appreciated the vital importance of the defensive boxes that lay around the perimeter of Tobruk, particularly the El Adem Box to the south of the port.

Auchinleck had already informed Ritchie that there was to be no repeat of the previous year's siege. The fortifications surrounding Tobruk had degenerated markedly during the intervening period, the garrison was weaker than it had previously been and the Royal Navy had made it clear that it would not be prepared

to suffer a large loss of shipping on resupply convoys. However, to Winston Churchill the retention of the port had become a matter of national prestige, regardless of the strategic merits of holding on to it. He constantly urged Auchinleck to prepare for another siege and on several occasions forbade any contemplation of withdrawal. These restrictions, placed on Auchinleck by a Prime Minister who had no idea of the day-to-day realities of the situation, contributed greatly to the subsequent capture of thousands of men who might otherwise have escaped.

Rommel felt that Tobruk would fall if only he could capture El Adem, Sidi

Rezegh and Gambut quickly. With DAK units poised to cut the Via Balbia east of the port, Ritchie would have either to order a hurried retreat or to face a mass surrender. Auchinleck also realised the importance of the position and ordered Ritchie to bring 'maximum force into play in the El Adem area'; to block Rommel successfully he would have to 'emulate the enemy's speed in thought and action . . . I wish you to impress this as strongly as possible on all commanders.' Unfortunately Ritchie failed on all counts.

On 15 June the 90th Light Division began its move on El Adem, while the 21st Panzer Division

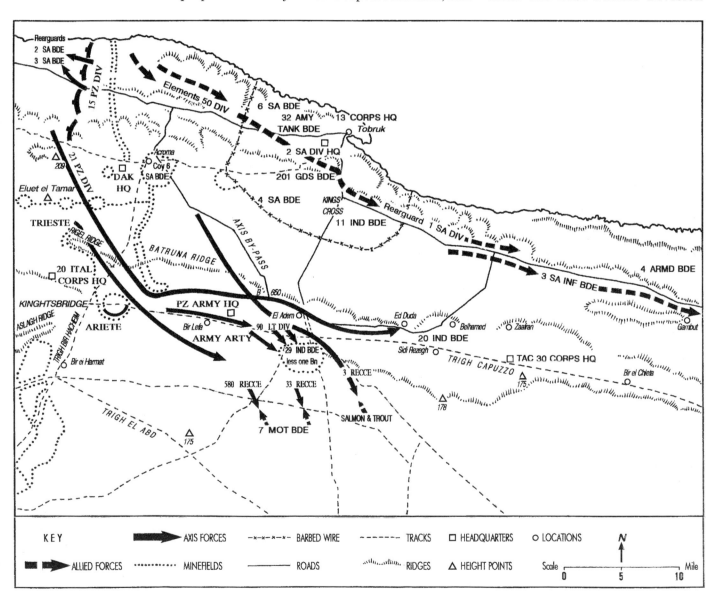

shifted its axis of advance, arriving from the Acroma area late in the afternoon and overrunning a box of the 3/12th Frontier Force Rifles trying to block the Tobruk by-pass road. It was a promising beginning to the next phase of the battle, and in his orders for 16 June Rommel ordered the 21st Panzer Division to push on to Sidi Rezegh and Belhamed, whilst the 90th Light Division, supported by the Panzerarmee's heavy artillery, was to attack the El Adem Box (held by two battalions of the 29th Indian Brigade). Meanwhile the Ariete Armoured Division and the three DAK reconnaissance units (3rd, 33rd and 580th) were to guard the southern flank of the advance against any interference from the 7th Motorised Brigade and other light forces based at Bir el Gubi. The 15th Panzer Division was to come up in support just as soon as the last pocket of South African resistance had been cleared from the area west of Tobruk.

On 16 June, while fighting raged for the El Adem Box, Ritchie once again ordered forward the 4th Armoured Brigade. Now up to 100 tanks in strength after receiving new vehicles, new crews, ammunition and petrol at the 8th Army dump at Gambut, it was sent forward to relieve the beleaguered Indians. The armour soon found its way blocked by an anti-tank gun screen thrown out by the 21st Panzer Division west of Zaafran to cover for just such an eventuality. Most of the replacement crews had never before been in combat and did not know how to address the tactical problem that had arisen, while the surviving veterans hung back, knowing just how deadly the enemy's guns (particularly his 88s) were. The result was a stand-off.

Behind this screen the tanks and mechanised infantry of the 21st Panzer Division methodically destroyed the 20th Indian Brigade boxes at Sidi Rezegh and Belhamed (elements of the brigade managed to fight on in the area until 18 June). The 29th Indian Brigade holding El Adem proved a much tougher nut to crack. Without tank support, the infantry of the 90th Light Division found it very difficult to break into the Indian

Below: An Italian artillery observation post, February 1942. (IWM MH5865)

defensive position. They had still not succeeded by nightfall when Rommel visited the area to assess the progress of the assault. General Marcks, the 90th Light's commanding officer, asked his superior for panzer support; Rommel refused, stating that all of his armour was needed for the next phase of his offensive. A sharp exchange of views followed, at the end of which Rommel agreed to let Marcks call off the attack.

Unfortunately for Ritchie, Brigadier Reid, commander of the 29th Indian Brigade, had also come to the conclusion that the fight could not be continued, and he requested and received permission to break out from the El Adem Box (despite the fact that Ritchie had earlier promised General H. B. Klopper, in charge of

the Tobruk garrison, that he would not allow any withdrawal). This the 29th Indian Brigade did in the early hours of 17 June.

The next morning Rommel continued his thrust to the north-east with a view to knocking out the 4th Armoured Brigade and opening up a route to Gambut. All three of the Panzerarmee's tank formations were present, the 15th Panzer Division and Ariete Armoured Division having moved up to join the 21st Panzer Division during the night. The armoured clash took place during the early afternoon to the south-east of Sidi Rezegh.

Despite a gallant effort from the novice British tank crews and the exhausted survivors of the Gazala battle, the odds against them were

just too great. The action soon developed into a running fight, with the British being pursued far to the south. At the end of the day's fighting they had lost over 50 tanks and had been forced back across the border into Egypt. Ritchie's last armoured reserve had gone. As darkness fell Rommel placed himself in the van of the Afrika Korps and headed north. Just after midnight DAK reached and crossed the Via Balbia near Gambut. Tobruk was cut off.

Below: A Grant tank of A Squadron, 4th County of London Yeomanry, receives a new supply of 75mm shells, 18 June 1942. The tank's used ammunition can be seen littering the ground. (IWM E13552)

While the German and Italian armour had been trouncing Ritchie's last hope for keeping a corridor to the port open, other Axis formations had been moving forward to the battle area. By the evening of 18 June Tobruk had been fully invested. The Italian XXI Corps was deployed to its west and X Corps to the south. The 90th Light Division and the three DAK reconnaissance battalions sealed the gap in the east. Rommel now prepared for his assault on Tobruk.

The attack was to begin at 5.20 a.m. on 20 June with a heavy artillery bombardment and Stuka attack on the positions of the 11th Indian Brigade, holding the south-eastern sector of the defences. Kampfgruppe Menny, a small mixed infantry formation made up of troops from all three German divisions, were ordered to penetrate gaps made by engineers in the perimeter minefields several hours before the main assault. They would then make a breach on a narrow front in the fortifications behind the main anti-tank ditch (in the sector held by the 2/5th Mahrattas). Meanwhile engineers following up behind were to bridge the ditch in preparation for the assault to follow. The 15th and 21st Panzer Divisions, with their panzers and mechanised infantry in the lead, were then to pour through the breach into the fortress interior.

Rommel was astonished to find that the ammunition dumps near El Adem, built up by the Germans in preparation for their planned Novem-

Left, upper: A Bersaglieri despatch rider arrives at a DAK headquarters unit. Note the SdKfz 263 Panzerfunkwagen complete with frame aerial. (IWM MH5567) Left, lower: A K-39 210mm heavy gun of Artillery Group 104 is prepared for action. (IWM MH6330) Right: Stukas in flight over Tobruk. (IWM MH5591)

Left: An LFH 18 105mm field gun
fires on British positions in
Tobruk, June 1942. (IWM MH5568)

anti-tank ditch bridged. The panzers and mechanised infantry poured through into the fortress interior.

The poor defence put up by the Indians was in part due, paradoxically, to the excellent Italian-built concrete bunkers in which they were deployed. The artillery fire and aerial bombing had driven the Mahrattas deep underground, where they took few casualties but were also unable to prevent the infantry of Kampfgruppe Menny working their way through the defences. Another major weakness was the lack of defensive support fire for the Indians. The 25th Field Regiment Royal Artillery, attached to the 11th Indian Brigade, had positioned their 25pdrs in an anti-tank role along the perimeter, leaving the medium guns of the 2nd South African Division to provide indirect artillery support. However, constant breakdowns in communication ensured that the first defensive artillery fire did not arrive until 7.45 a.m., after the breach in the perimeter had been made. The fire did not become heavy until over an hour later, by which time most of the German armour had passed through.

ber 1941 attack on Tobruk, had been left intact and in position. This oversight on the part of the Allies enabled DAK to move straight into the attack without having to wait for its logistical tail to catch up.

The Tobruk perimeter was guarded by the 4th South African Brigade (western sector), 6th South African Brigade (southern sector) and 11th Indian Brigade (south-eastern sector). In reserve, positioned on the Pilastrino Ridge in the centre of the defences, were the 201st Guards Brigade, and behind them were deployed the 52 remaining Matilda and Valentine tanks of the 32nd Army Tank Brigade.

At 5.20 a.m. Kesselring's air support arrived over the battlefield and hundreds of Axis bombers blasted the defensive positions of the 11th Indian Brigade. The screaming sirens of the Stukas were soon joined by the explosions of artillery fire from the heavy guns of Artillery Group 104.

At just after 6 a.m. the assault engineers of Menny's detachment released orange smoke as a signal that the bombardment should be moved back into the fortress interior. At 6.35 a.m. the leading troops reported that they were through the wire and attacking the forward line of bunkers; at 7.03 a.m. Menny signalled back that a company of Indians had been taken prisoner; and by 7.45 a.m. a wide breach had been made and the

Right: Italian field artillery fires on Allied positions. (IWM HU28365)

Nevertheless, there was still time for the Allies to mount a coordinated counter-attack with their plentiful reserves, which might have plugged the breach. Unfortunately, although Klopper had had the sense to create a central reserve (201st Guards Brigade and 32nd Army Tank Brigade), he had not put together a plan with which to use them.

At 7 a.m., as the battle unfolded, Klopper had ordered forward the 4th RTR and two companies of the 3rd Battalion Coldstream Guards to aid the Indians. This small force would have been insufficient for the task even if it had carried through a well-rehearsed counter-attack, but, as sadly happened all too often, the move broke down. The 4th RTR did not reach King's Cross, the road junction jumping-off point for the attack,

until 9.30 a.m., by which time the German panzers and half-tracks had fanned out and were well inside the perimeter. To their surprise, the tankers found that even though they were late the Guards were even later and had not as yet turned up. Realising that if they delayed for much longer the panzers would be upon them in their present positions in the centre of the Tobruk defences, the Matildas and Valentines pressed on. So, yet again, a British attack petered out into a piecemeal débâcle, units being committed to action without adequate support (the Guards companies, when they did finally arrive, did not move forward and stayed at King's Cross).

The 7th RTR did attempt to intervene on receiving radioed messages for help from the 4th RTR, but it, too,

committed the cardinal sin of pushing forward its tanks in dribs and drabs, the two remaining squadrons of the regiment being sent into battle one after the other instead of deploying in one mass. As a consequence, the German panzers faced for several hours an almost continuous stream of attacking British armour, but the assaults were not coordinated, had little artillery and no air

Below: Knocked-out armoured cars and a destroyed A13 cruiser tank litter a Tobruk side street after the capture of the port by the DAK, June 1942. Note that the tank still carries the 2nd Armoured Division's plumed helmet insignia, even though the division had been disbanded after Operation 'Sunflower' over a year earlier. (IWM MH5560)

Above: Allied prisoners are marched to the rear after the fall of Tobruk, June 1942. (IWM MH5577)

support and all were woefully under-strength. By 2 p.m. the armoured battle was over, the battlefield was littered with knocked-out British tanks and the leading elements of DAK had reached the escarpment in the centre of the Tobruk position.

During the morning's critical fighting not one senior officer of the 2nd South African Division, 32nd Army Tank Brigade or 201st Guards Brigade had been present anywhere near the breach or the King's Cross fighting. With such inadequate leadership it is no wonder that the Germans viewed the break in battle as an easy victory.

With DAK firmly established in the middle of the Allied positions, the battle for Tobruk was for all practical purposes over. All that remained was for the Germans to mop up the last few areas of resistance inside the

perimeter. During the afternoon the 15th Panzer Division advanced against the Guards on Pilastrino Ridge, and by the end of the day they had overwhelmed the 1st Battalion Sherwood Foresters and the 3rd Battalion Coldstream Guards and captured the headquarters of the 201st Guards Brigade. Meanwhile the 21st Panzer Division advanced against Tobruk harbour, its main opposition coming from anti-aircraft units hurriedly converted into an anti-tank defence. As dusk was falling the first German units fought their way into Tobruk town and opened fire on the remaining naval vessels still in the harbour.

While the panzer divisions created chaos inside the perimeter, the Ariete Division followed up the assault, methodically cleaning out the remaining strongpoints still held by the 11th Indian Brigade. By the evening of 20 June the only area of the Tobruk perimeter still in Allied hands lay to the west and south-west of the port. In

this small enclave were crammed the remaining combat troops of the 4th and 6th South African Brigades and the many thousands of rear-echelon personal who had fled westwards from Tobruk on its fall.

General Klopper attempted to gain permission from Ritchie and Auchinleck to break out during the night, but poor radio communications meant that he failed to get a coherent reply, and, displaying the same lack of initiative which had been apparent amongst other Allied field commanders earlier in the campaign, he therefore did nothing at all.

Shortly after dawn on 21 June, his chance of escape now gone, Klopper ordered the Tobruk garrison to surrender and 33,000 Allied troops, huge dumps of food, ammunition and fuel and hundreds of serviceable guns and vehicles fell into Rommel's hands. Later that evening the Panzerarmee commander heard over the radio that he had been promoted to Field Marshal by a grateful *Führer*.

CHAPTER SEVEN

THE BEGINNING OF THE END

Even though Rommel had decisively beaten the 8th Army, difficult and far-reaching strategic decisions had yet to be taken regarding the future conduct of the campaign in North Africa. These decisions, and not the previous conduct of Panzerarmee Afrika on the field of battle, would ultimately seal the fate of the Axis in the theatre.

At the end of April 1942 Mussolini and Hitler had, on the advice of their respective military staffs, agreed that the advance in North Africa would come to a halt as soon as Tobruk had fallen. All available *Luftwaffe* and *Kriegsmarine* resources were then to be diverted to support Operation 'Hercules', the planned invasion of Malta. The island fortress had long been a thorn in Rommel's side. British submarines, surface vessels and aircraft had incessantly raided the Italian supply convoys to Tripoli and Benghazi, severely disrupting Panzerarmee Afrika's ability to wage war against the 8th Army. On many occasions Axis formations had ground to a halt because of a lack of fuel, or had been restricted in their

Below: Tripoli harbour after an RAF raid, 1941; the bodies of at least six dockers can be seen lying in the foreground. Raids such as these severely disrupted Rommel's flow of supplies and were a major factor in turning the tide of the campaign. (IWM HU70608)

attacking options by a shortfall of equipment or ammunition.

The situation got worse as Rommel neared the Egyptian/Libyan frontier. In order to sustain a deep thrust into the Egyptian interior it would be necessary to bring in much of the Axis supplies through Tobruk (Tripoli was too far to the rear and Benghazi had only a limited shipping capacity). This in turn would mean Axis convoys having to travel closer both to Malta and to the other main Royal Navy base in the Mediterranean, Alexandria. Undoubtedly shipping losses would increase, probably to an unsustainable level. So it had been decided that Malta would have to be captured before any advance to the Suez Canal could be contemplated.

On the day Tobruk fell Kesselring arrived at Panzerarmee Headquarters to inform Rommel that *Luftwaffe* units currently supporting the advance were to be withdrawn to Sicily in preparation for the attack on Malta. Rommel, who knew of and had in the past reluctantly agreed to limit his offensive until the island had fallen, was incensed by the news. He argued that the Panzerarmee now had a unique opportunity to deliver a fatal blow to the Allies in North Africa, and that although his forces had sustained severe losses he must push on. Kesselring was unmoved and departed for the rear, leaving Rommel in no doubt that as far as the *Luftwaffe* was concerned the original German High Command restrictions on his operations still stood.

The Panzerarmee commander was never a man to take no for an answer and reacted to the news, as he had done in the past, by appealing directly to Mussolini and Hitler. This tactic had in the past brought him success and it worked this time too. After telling his political masters that 'the state and morale of the troops, the present supply situation owing to captured dumps, and the present

weakness of the enemy permit our pursuing him into the depths of the Egyptian area', he received a message from the *Führer* granting Rommel permission to continue with the offensive, saying, 'It is only once in a lifetime that the Goddess of Victory smiles.' The invasion of Malta was postponed and all available resources were directed back towards the desert campaign.

This may have suited Rommel, but it was entirely the wrong decision. Rommel undoubtedly inflated the strength of his position in his communications with the Fascist and Nazi leadership to get the answers he wanted. Morale was high, the enemy was weak and much fuel had been captured, but the Panzerarmee desperately needed reinforcements of both men and tanks. Without them it stood little chance of capturing Egypt, the Allies' last stronghold.

Overconfidence had once again got the better of Rommel's judgement. Just as he had ordered the ill-fated 'Dash to the Wire' during Operation 'Crusader', in the belief that a battered Afrika Korps could beat a numerically larger Allied force through

Above: A PzKpfw III of the 8th Panzer Regiment drops off a wounded infantryman picked up on the battlefield at a DAK field hospital, May/June 1942. (IWM HU60348)

superior tactics alone, he now believed that a similarly depleted Panzerarmee Afrika could carry the day against Auchinleck's dispirited forces. And for a little while it looked as though he was right.

In the evening of 23 June the Afrika Korps' advance guard crossed the border into Egypt. Rommel had expected the heavily fortified frontier zone to be stoutly defended by the Allies but Ritchie had already ordered a general withdrawal to Matruh. This was fortunate for DAK as the previous weeks of fighting had reduced its panzer strength to only 44 vehicles, and any serious resistance by the Allies might well have brought the advance to a standstill. As it was, the Axis forces were able to pursue the retiring Allied formations for over 100 miles until, in the evening of 25 June, they came to a halt at the outer defences of Mersa Matruh.

Although DAK had received little in the way of attention from Allied ground forces during the advance, there had been a marked increase in Desert Air Force activity against the DAK columns. The pace of the pursuit was fast outstripping the ability of the *Luftwaffe* and *Regia Aeronautica* to keep up—and the further Rommel could be tempted into Egypt the more aircraft the 8th Army had available to support it, flying from permanent bases on the Nile delta. The Axis formations were never again to enjoy the advantage of even temporary air superiority over the battlefield, and this was a major factor in the reverse to come. To make matters even worse, over the next few weeks the Allies introduced new types of tank-busting aircraft and light bombers to the battlefield, greatly enhancing the Desert Air Force's ability to provide effective battlefield support and tilting the air war irrevocably in favour of the Allies.

On 25 June Auchinleck decided, rather belatedly, to remove Ritchie from command of the 8th Army. A good staff officer he may well have been, but army command was too much for him. Unable to find anyone in whom he had confidence to step into his shoes immediately, Auchinleck decided to take control

himself, announcing that he would be taking on the dual role of Commander-in-Chief Middle East and 8th Army Command until a suitable replacement could be found.

Things did not begin auspiciously for the new commander. Rommel, still believing he was pursing an enemy with little will to fight, decided to attack Mersa Matruh the next day. He had arrived at nightfall in front of the enemy position and there had been little time for reconnaissance, and as a result the attack was to go in blind. DAK intelligence assumed that five Allied divisions were in the area—four infantry divisions (the 50th British, the 2nd New Zealand and the 5th and 10th Indian) and one armoured division (1st Armoured Division). The infantry formations, Rommel thought, would most likely be deployed in a line south from

Matruh, with their left flank resting on the Sidi Hamza escarpment. The 1st Armoured Division would probably be held as a reserve to the south or south-east of the escarpment to cover any outflanking manoeuvre through the desert by German panzers. To counter this Rommel proposed not to conduct a wide sweep around the end of the Allied line, as he had done previously, but to force a passage just north of the escarpment. This would, he hoped, cut off the Allied infantry from their supporting armour, thereby forcing a British tank counter-attack, which would once again fall on well-prepared panzers and anti-tank guns in defensive positions. It would be a battle the British were bound to lose.

It was estimated that the 1st Armoured Division possessed 100 tanks, whilst DAK entered the bat-

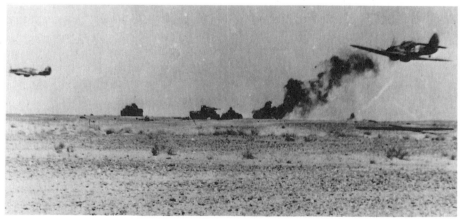

Right, upper: Four Baltimore II medium bombers of No 55 Squadron RAF on their way to attack Axis troop concentrations, May 1942. (IWM K3854)
Right, lower: Hurricane Mk IID aircraft, of No 6 Squadron RAF, armed with twin Vickers 40mm cannon sweep in to attack German armour, May/June 1942. With the arrival of these dedicated 'tank buster' aircraft in North Africa from February 1942 the panzers rapidly began to lose the battlefield ascendancy they had held since April 1941. (IWM MH7460)

Above: The Battle of Mersa Matruh, 26–27 June 1942.

tle with only 66 servicable panzers. Therefore Rommel could only win an armoured engagement by drawing the British on to an anti-tank screen (in fact the 1st Armoured Division was 159 tanks strong, 60 of them Grants with 75mm guns). In reality the Allies had not deployed in the manner expected of them: they had in fact been drawn up in an unconventional formation that proved even easier to crack. X Corps (50th Infantry Division and 10th Indian Division) was deployed in and around Mersa Matruh as expected, but XIII Corps (2nd New Zealand Division and 1st Armoured Division) was deployed south of the Sidi Hamza escarpment, thus leaving a ten-mile gap in the centre of the Allied line.

Covering this gap were two *ad hoc* Jock Columns, Leathercol and Gleecol, each consisting of two platoons of infantry and a battery each of field and anti-tank artillery. Even though their positions were defended by a wide belt of mines, there were simply not enough troops in this central sector of the Allied defence line to hold anything but the lightest of attacks. Unfortunately for the unsupported soldiers of the 29th Indian Brigade who made up the Jock Columns, this is precisely where Rommel launched his main assault.

While the 90th Light Division and the 21st Panzer Division smashed through the south-centre of the Allied line, the 15th Panzer Division, accompanied by the Italian Ariete and Trieste Divisions, was ordered to push eastwards along the southern edge of the Sidi Hamza escarpment,

in an attempt to find and pin the 1st Armoured Division, to stop any premature interference with the panzer thrust in the centre. At the same time the infantry divisions of the Italian XXI Corps advanced against the Allied defences west and south of Matruh in an attempt to hold the Allied infantry in position while the outflanking manoeuvre was carried through.

Left, upper: A squadron of Grant tanks on the move, 17 February 1942. (IWM E8467)
Right: A British supply column under air attack, 16 June 1942. (IWM E13498)
Far right: General Georg von Bismarck (left), commander of the 21st Panzer Division, consults with an aide during the post-Gazala pursuit, June/July 1942. (IWM HU22338)

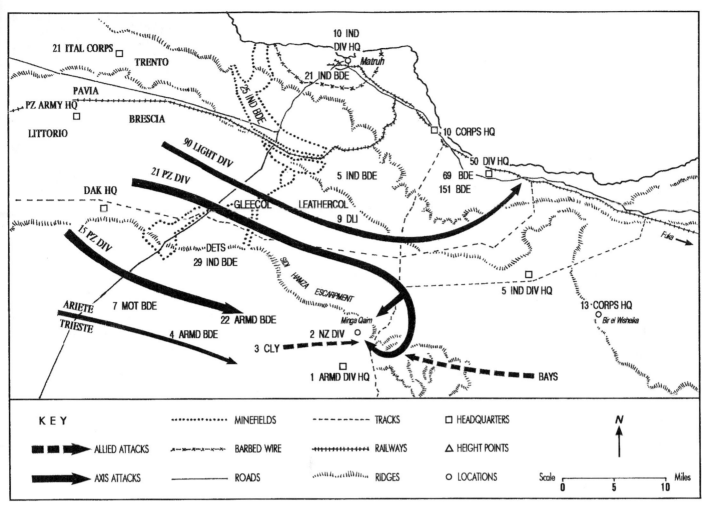

KEY

············· MINEFIELDS
- - - - - - TRACKS
□ HEADQUARTERS
∎∎∎➤ ALLIED ATTACKS
-x-x-x-x-x- BARBED WIRE
+++++++++ RAILWAYS
△ HEIGHT POINTS
➤ AXIS ATTACKS
——— ROADS
⌣⌣⌣⌣ RIDGES
○ LOCATIONS

N

Scale
0   5   10   Miles

The attack began in the afternoon of 26 June, the 90th Light Division penetrating the Allied minefields with relative ease and annihilating Leathercol in the briefest of engagements; at the same time, a few miles further west, the 21st Panzer Division did likewise to Gleecol. With the enemy centre ruptured, the way was open for a deep thrust into the Allied rear the following day.

At dawn on 27 June the 90th Light Division overran a defensive box held by the 9th Battalion Durham Light Infantry which for some inexplicable reason had been set up some 17 miles south of Matruh, well away from any supporting ground units. At the same time the 21st Panzer Division moved across the northern flank of the 2nd New Zealand Division at Minqa Qaim, then swept south and southeast to hit the formation in the rear. This risky manoeuvre left the German panzer division's line of communication to the rear completely unprotected, and liable to be cut at any time. Matters were made potentially worse by the fact that Rommel insisted he be in the van of the attack with the 21st Panzer Division: a British thrust to the north by the 1st Armoured Division or south by the 50th Infantry Division would not only have bagged half of DAK's remaining panzers but also their commander-in-chief.

The division could also have been relatively easily destroyed by XIII Corps had they put in a combined armoured/infantry counter-attack larger than brigade size, the 21st Panzer Division being able to field only 23 panzers and 600 mechanised infantry. XIII Corps could have faced them with three times that number of vehicles and men and still have had more than enough in reserve to hold off the Italian and German formations moving against them from the west. Fortunately for Rommel, the British armour failed to cooper-

ate effectively with the New Zealand infantry and the majority of the 1st Armoured Division deployed to face the oncoming 15th Panzer and Ariete Armoured Divisions, only the Bays and the 3rd County of London Yeomanry putting in unsupported charges against 21st Panzer Division positions, which as usual foundered on well-placed anti-tank gun screens. Nevertheless, things looked bleak for the division by nightfall: it was low on ammunition and almost out of fuel, and a sizeable attack by any force the next day might have spelt the end for it.

In the afternoon of 27 June Rommel had moved north and joined the 90th Light Division (at this time the formation had no panzers attached and consisted of 1,600 motorised infantry with anti-tank gun support). Under his supervision the formation swung round the southern flank of X Corps' defensive positions, cutting the coast road at nightfall, some 20 miles south-east of Matruh. Although DAK had two of its formations deep in the enemy's rear, strad-

dling their lines of retreat, Auchinleck had a great opportunity to turn and defeat these units in detail and swing the battle back in his favour. The 90th Light Division and the 21st Panzer Division were more than 15 miles apart, understrength and low on fuel and ammunition, and with a very tenuous line of communication to the rear.

Unfortunately for the 8th Army Commander, the nerve of General Gott, in command of XIII Corps, gave way. In the afternoon of 27 June, with three Axis divisions to his front and one to his rear (the fact that all four added together were significantly smaller than his force does not seem to have been taken into account), he ordered a general withdrawal to the rear. To make matters worse, Gott failed to transmit his intentions directly to X Corps in the north, with the result that they did not find out about the retreat until 4.30 p.m. the next day, when they were told by 8th Army Headquarters.

During the night of 27/28 June the 1st Armoured Division pulled back across the southern flank of the 21st Panzer Division but the New Zealanders retreated straight through the formation, inflicting serious losses on its remaining infantry. This indicates just what might have been achieved had any effort been made to mount a sustained attack on the German position. During 28 June, while the 21st Panzer Division kept in touch with the retreating XIII Corps, the 90th Light Division and the Italian infantry divisions of XXI Corps invested Matruh (the 15th Panzer and the Ariete and Trieste Divisions followed in the 21st Panzer's wake as best they could).

The delay in making known XIII Corps' retreat to X Corps was to cost the Allies dear. Twenty-four hours earlier a withdrawal by X Corps could have taken place with relative ease, but now the 50th Infantry Division and 10th Indian Division would have to break through a solid line of Axis troops. This they did during the night of 28/29 June. Many units managed to escape, largely due to the weakness of the surrounding Axis formations, but over 8,000 men fell into Rommel's hands. Mersa Matruh was entered by troops of the 90th Light Division in the morning of 29 June.

Further east, the 21st Panzer Division managed to round up another 1,600, mostly rear echelon, prisoners. The Battle of Mersa Matruh had been a decisive victory for Rommel, gained largely because of the ineptitude and

lack of confidence prevalent amongst the senior British commanders involved in the fighting. The battle proved to Winston Churchill that Auchinleck could not cope with the dual responsibility of army and theatre command and that he needed to be replaced (Churchill's first and very dubious choice for his successor was Gott). However, before the change of command could be carried through another engagement was fought, this time near El Alamein, which brought the Axis advance to a halt.

Rommel's divisional commanders were dismayed when they heard that

Below: : Bren Carriers of the 9th Battalion The Rifle Brigade pause to watch the destruction of a large British supply dump during the retreat to the Alamein Line, 1942. (IWM E14010)

their leader intended to push on yet again and bounce the Allies out of another defensive position. They were acutely aware of the parlous state of the formations they commanded, and most felt that a halt at the Matruh Line to rest, recuperate and receive reinforcements of men and equipment was necessary before any further advance could be contemplated. However, Rommel realised that the Allies would receive reinforcements at a much faster rate than he would, and that they would be able to deploy and use them much earlier because of the vast difference in length of the opposing armies' lines of communication. His only hope was

a quick thrust which might keep the Allies off balance and open the road to Alexandria. This was a very risky undertaking. If it failed not only would the advance grind to a halt, but Rommel would be left with a non-battleworthy army that could easily be forced to flee back to Tripolitania or even be made to surrender. The further Rommel advanced the clearer it became that waiting at Tobruk for the fall of Malta would have been the wiser option.

Rommel, however, was never a man to question his own decisions, and he ordered Panzerarmee Afrika to press on. During 29 June the pursuit of the Allied forces continued, the

Above: A New Zealand machine-gun post in a rocky outcrop on the Alamein Line, July 1942. (IWM E14536)

only minor clash taking place between the advance guard of the 21st Panzer Division and the rearguard of the 1st Armoured Division just before dark. The remainder of the Panzerarmee's motorised and mechanised units camped down alongside the 21st Panzer Division some 15 miles from the Alamein Line after dark. The Italian infantry divisions followed as best they could, strung out along the coast road. As well as the units from XIII Corps that had pulled back from Matruh (those who had escaped from X Corps were in no condition to make a stand), the Alamein Line was manned by the 5th Indian Division, the 7th Armoured Division and the 1st South African Division, many of whose units were understrength (but rested), although two brigades (6th New Zealand and 18th Indian) were at full complement.

During 30 June Rommel drew up his plan of attack. Realising that his units were in no condition to undertake protracted fighting, he intended to repeat the manoeuvre that had brought him victory at Matruh. During the night of 30 June/1 July DAK moved to a start line some ten miles to the south-west of El Alamein station. Rommel's plan was to thrust between the defensive boxes at Alamein and Deir el Abyad and push on into the rear of XIII Corps, which was thought to be holding the area southeast of the break-through point. It was hoped that Gott would be panicked into ordering another precipitate withdrawal, leaving XXX Corps no choice but to fall back from the northern sector of the defence line (as had happened to X Corps at Matruh).

However, things went wrong from the start of the attack. At dawn on 1 July DAK discovered that there was no Allied defensive box at Deir el Abyad, but that the 18th Indian Brigade was holding a box three miles further east at Deir el Shein. It was still possible to by-pass this new position to move into the rear of XIII Corps, but it would mean pushing DAK further east before they could move south, in which case they would have to cross the well-defended Ruweisat Ridge. Auchinleck had for once deployed his troops very astutely. Nehring, placed on the horns of a dilemma, decided that it would be easier to eliminate the Deir el Shein Box than it would be to capture Ruweisat Ridge. Rommel, arriv-

ing on the battlefield in mid-morning, backed his judgement.

During the afternoon of 1 July DAK broke into the Deir el Shein Box, and after very fierce fighting destroyed the 18th Indian Brigade. However, the full-strength Indian formation inflicted very heavy casualties on the Germans, knocking out 18 of DAK's 55 remaining panzers. While the fighting at Deir el Shein raged, the 90th Light Division probed eastwards to see if a passage could be found into XIII Corps' rear through by-passing Ruweisat Ridge. However, the dramatically below strength and extremely tired units of the division soon became pinned down by heavy and accurate fire from the 1st and 2nd South African Brigades, and this reverse was only prevented from turning into a rout by the personal intervention of Rommel. It was clear from the battlefield behaviour of this élite German formation that DAK had reached the end of its tether. The panzer divisions, having been drawn into a battle of attrition for the Deir el Shein Box—just the thing Rommel wanted to avoid—were too exhausted to press on, and the attempted advance did not resume until the next day. Rommel still hoped that an easy way

through the British defence line could be found which might turn the tide of the engagement. However, it was not to be.

On 2 July the advancing panzers ran into a counter-attack from the 22nd Armoured Brigade and wave upon wave of Desert Air Force bombers. No way could be found through the defence line that would not have entailed the almost complete destruction of the already decimated attacking force. The next day, with the Littorio Armoured Division in support, DAK tried one last time to hammer a way through the South African defences. However, as Rommel had long suspected, the battlefield effectiveness of Italian units (with the notable exceptions of the Ariete and Trieste Divisions) was worse than that of his German formations, even though they had seen less fighting and had taken far fewer casualties. The attack failed. That evening Rommel signalled to Kesselring that he had been forced to suspend his advance 'for the time being'. It was now a matter of hanging on while the Allies attempted to turn the check

Below: DAK panzers push on into Egypt, early July 1942. (IWM HU40255)

they had delivered to DAK's advance into a rout.

In the morning of 4 July DAK could call on 36 panzers and a few hundred exhausted infantrymen. There was little fuel and the Corps' artillery and tanks were nearly out of ammunition (the 15th Panzer Division had only two rounds per gun). The Italian artillery and tanks were more plentifully supplied, but Rommel was loath to use them in any quantity in front-line positions, fearing a mass rout on first contact with the enemy. The Italian troops, like the Germans, were utterly ex-hausted, but, unlike their Axis part-ners, they were beginning actively to contemplate surrender. Fortunately for Rommel a large Allied counter-attack did not develop on 4 July, de-spite Auchinleck having ordered one. The Allied troops were also tired, and, more importantly, they were down-hearted; they feared that an attack would leave them open to a German counter-thrust, which would lead to disaster, as had happened all too of-ten in the past. They preferred to sit tight and wait.

On 5 July, after constant urging from Auchinleck for something to be

Above: The wounded driver of a lorry destroyed by German air attack is helped away from his vehicle, 5 July 1942. The truck contained aviation spirit being taken forward to resupply a unit of Stuart light tanks. (IWM E13998)

done, the 4th New Zealand Brigade moved off to attack the southern flank of the German defences. How-ever, the Brigade Headquarters was caught in the open by a Stuka patrol and was destroyed. This was all that was needed for higher authority to abandon the assault, and the front once more lapsed into stalemate.

On 6 July a supply column reached DAK laden with mines, some German infantry reinforcements and eight panzers. Rommel used the mines to strengthen his defensive positions and used the tanks as the basis of a mobile reserve. Three days later the ever-cautious Allies had still not taken advantage of their numerical superiority; in fact they strengthened Rommel's hand by abandoning the Qarat el Abd Box, allowing DAK to enhance its flank defence further by occupying the abandoned position.

Finally, on 10 July the 9th Australian Division, new to the battle front, opened up a major offensive along the coast road against the Sabratha Division. The Italians put up a brief resistance and then fled. There was then nothing between the Australian vanguard and the Axis rear but Panzerarmee Headquarters, stationed a few miles behind the front line on the coast. Rommel was away, overseeing the fortification of the newly acquired Qarat el Abd Box, and the holding of the Allied thrust fell upon Lieutenant-Colonel F. W. von Mellenthin, his chief of intelligence. The headquarters staff and its anti-aircraft guns were deployed

Above: South African infantry man a Vickers machine gun in the Alamein Box, 4 July 1942. (IWM E13981)

across the coast road and they successfully held the initial Australian attack, although they took heavy casualties, including most of the members of Rommel's excellent and irreplaceable Wireless Intercept Company.

Again, good fortune was on Rommel's side. As the fighting raged a relief column from the west arrived along the coast road. Containing the

main body of the 382nd Infantry Regiment, the lead unit of the 164th Infantry Division and the first German reinforcement formation despatched to Africa for several months, it soon brought the Australian assault to a halt. The Allies had launched their attack one day too late.

They tried again the next day, this time thrusting south-westwards against the Trieste Division. Once again Italian resistance began to crumble almost immediately, and only prompt action by Panzerarmee artillery saved the day, the heavy guns of Artillery Group 104 putting down a blanket of fire which halted the advance. The 9th Australian Division, unsupported by its battle-weary sister formations, then suspended its attack.

The next day Rommel decided that it was time to launch an attack of his own. He hoped that by assaulting the El Alamein Box he could advance to the coast road and cut off a large number of the Australians who had so recently threatened to break through the Axis line. Unfortunately for the 21st Panzer Division, who launched the attack, the coordinated timing of artillery and *Luftwaffe* support for the assault went awry. Because of this, unsuppressed Allied

Left, upper: A New Zealand soldier wounded during the fighting on Ruweisat Ridge is stretchered into a waiting American field service ambulance, 15 July 1942. (IWM E14611)
Left, lower: Two severely dehydrated Italian prisoners captured on Ruweisat Ridge, 15 July 1942. They had been without supplies for three days. (IWM E14622)
Right, upper: A 4.5 inch howitzer fires on the advancing Axis, 20 July 1942. (IWM E14639)
Right, lower: New Zealanders let fly at a Stuka buzzing their truck, 17 July 1942. (IWM E14530)

artillery was able to fire on the attackers, separating the dismounted infantry from the mechanised armour and effectively halting the advance. Rommel tried again the next day but was rebuffed once more. On 14 July the axis of the 21st Panzer Division's advance was shifted so that it fell not upon the fortifications

Left: An armoured car of the 12th Lancers on observation duty near New Zealand positions south of the Alamein Box, 20 July 1942. (IWM E14640)
Below: A Crusader tank of the 22nd Armoured Brigade, 28 July 1942. (IWM E14950)

of the Alamein Box but on the junction between it and the 26th Australian Infantry Brigade positioned to its west. This assault reached the coastal railway line but was unable to proceed any further because of intense flanking fire laid down by the 3rd South African Brigade from the Alamein Box. Reluctantly Rommel called off the attacks.

On 15 July the Allies struck again. This time the 2nd New Zealand Division and the 5th Indian Brigade attacked the Brescia Division on Ruweisat Ridge. As was now usual, the Italian formation shattered under the impact and for a while the Allies

threatened to break the Axis defence line in two. But the New Zealanders failed to follow up on their success and settled for holding on to the ground gained from the Italians. This gave Rommel time to organise a counter-attack by the 15th Panzer Division and the 3rd and 33rd Reconnaissance Battalions which restored the situation. The day ended with the *status quo* reintroduced, the New Zealanders with 2,000 Italian prisoners and the Germans with 1,200 Indian and New Zealand troops captured.

On 16 and 17 July the 9th Australian Division tried once more to push

Above: A sIG self-propelled gun of Panzer Unit 707 in front of the Alamein position, August 1942. This is a very unusual photograph in that it shows a sIG based on a PzKpfw III chassis. As all the unit's original vehicles were manufactured from PzKpfw IIs, this particular sIG must have been an *ad hoc* field conversion, to replace battle losses. (IWM HU66481)

Below: Winston Churchill and Field Marshal Sir Alan Brooke (Chief of the Imperial General Staff) drive past British positions at Tel el Kebir during the Prime Minister's whistle-stop tour of the Middle East, 9 August 1942. (IWM E15387)

west, and when that failed south-west, from their Tell el Eisa positions west of the Alamein Box. It was highly optimistic of Auchinleck to hope that almost exact replicas of earlier failed attacks would succeed against the Axis positions, and, sure enough, DAK was more than ready to meet them. The assault was re-buffed. There was then a lull until the night of 21/22 July, when the 161st Indian Brigade and the 6th New Zealand Brigade attacked down the length of Ruweisat Ridge towards El Mireir. The attack went well and by the morning of 22 July the New Zealanders were firmly in possession of the El Mireir depression, well inside the Axis lines.

However, to hold against the expected panzer counter-attack (both the 15th and the 21st Panzer Divisions were in the vicinity) tank support was vitally needed. The 23rd Armoured Brigade, new to North Africa, had been assigned to provide the

Above: The commander of an armoured car of the 12th Lancers keeps a sharp look-out for enemy movements while on patrol, 10 August 1942. (IWM E15509)
Right: A 6pdr anti-tank gun in action, 11 August 1942. (IWM E15560)

New Zealanders with armoured support. They provided it the only way British armour seemed to know how—by a headlong charge against well-sited German anti-tank guns. The result was a complete disaster. British tank commanders had still had not learned their lesson. Counter-attacked by the 15th and 21st Panzer Divisions, the infantry were forced to withdraw. Once again, owing to poor inter-arms cooperation an

Above: A 5.5in howitzer lets fly at an enemy position, 14 August 1942. (IWM E15624)

Left: British 25pdr field guns receive counter-battery fire from a German position upon which they themselves are firing, 26 August 1942. (IWM E16114)

attack had failed. DAK captured 1,400 prisoners and knocked out over 100 precious British tanks in the engagement.

A last attempt was made by Auchinleck to resume the offensive during the night of 26/27 July. The 9th Australian Division once again thrust south-west, this time with the support of the 3rd South African Brigade. They had the limited objective of opening up a path through the German minefields, along which the British 69th Infantry Brigade and 1st Armoured Division were to pass, into the heart of the Axis defences.

The initial phase of the plan went well, the Australians capturing Sanyet el Miteiriya and the South Africans clearing the minefields as planned. The 69th Infantry Brigade duly passed through and forged on into the interior of the enemy position. At this point it all went wrong. The 1st Armoured Division refused to follow because in the opinion of its commander, Brigadier Fisher (Lumsden having been wounded), the lanes cleared through the minefields were not wide enough for his vehicles to proceed safely. As a result the 69th Infantry Brigade was left without support and suffered catastrophic losses when counter-attacked by panzers and German troops of the 200th Infantry Regiment. After the failure of this assault, fighting died down on the Alamein front. Auchinleck realised that his chance of inflicting a defeat through piecemeal attacks had passed. DAK had just managed to hold on.

Time was now needed to build up a strong Allied force and put together a coherent plan of attack for a new offensive. For Rommel the problem was quite different. He knew he would not be given the massive resources necessary for a major offensive, at least not without a significant battlefield success. Instead his options were to retire back to Cyrenaica and cut his losses (something that neither Hitler nor Mussolini would countenance) or gamble on another assault against a well dug-in enemy who outnumbered him and who had air superiority, in the hope of a collapse in Allied morale (as had hap-

Right, upper: A Stuart light tank of the 4th Hussars on patrol near Mount Himeimat at the southern end of the Alamein position, 26 August 1942. (IWM E16095)
Right, lower: Men of the 4th County of London Yeomanry bed down next to their Crusader tanks, 28 August 1942. (IWM E16262)

pened at Mersa Matruh). Rommel's natural inclination was to attack, which was just as well because he really had no other option.

The Panzerarmee Staff were dubious from the very beginning of the possibility for success of yet another offensive. The Axis supply situation was extremely tenuous. Rommel was now paying the price for pushing on when he should have halted and waited for the invasion of Malta. DAK intelligence estimated that the Allies had a superiority of 3:1 in armour and 5:1 in combat aircraft (both of these were incorrect: at the time of the Alam Halfa assault the actual ratio was more like 2:1 in both cases). Nevertheless, being outnumbered and attacking a well dug-in enemy emplaced behind wide belts of mines with tired troops, being low on ammunition and food and being critically short of fuel were not a recipe for success. Even if Rommel were to succeed in breaking through the Allied defence line and force a retreat he would probably not have enough fuel to allow him to follow up on his battlefield success (this situation was exacerbated when on 31 August an oil tanker on which the Axis were relying was sunk off Tobruk by a British submarine).

The situation was made worse for the Axis when the British reorganised their command structure. For

Left, upper: A mixed Italian/ German gun crew manhandles an Italian artillery piece into position. As the desert campaign wore on more and more German soldiers found themselves assigned to Italian units. They provided technical knowledge and training that their allies lacked and bolstered morale, keeping suspect formations battleworthy. (IWM HU32745)
Left, lower: A DAK sapper lifts an Allied mine during the preparations for the Alam Halfa thrust, August 1942. (IWM MH5863)

the first time since 1940 a thoroughly competent general was placed in charge of the Allied forces in North Africa. Bernard Law Montgomery only succeeded to command of the 8th Army on the tragic death of 'Strafer' Gott, Churchill's nominated replacement of Auchinleck. However, it soon became clear that this North African novice was just the man needed for the job. Without any false preconceptions about the 'true nature' of desert warfare, he brought to the 8th Army a fresh outlook, untainted by previous battlefield failures and full of confidence.

Montgomery arrived in North Africa on 12 August 1942. The next day he travelled out to the 8th Army's forward tactical HQ and was dismayed to find it within artillery range of enemy positions, far removed from Desert Air Force HQ. Worse than that, the whole place had an atmosphere of defeat. Officers thought not in terms of attack or even of defence but of falling back to the Nile delta should Rommel advance again. Montgomery was so alarmed that he decided to flout orders given to him by the outgoing commander Auchinleck, and took command immediately, two days before he was authorised to do so. All previous plans for withdrawal were scrapped and orders that the 8th Army was to stand fast and fight, and if necessary die, where it stood were issued. For the next two weeks, whilst Rommel busily scraped together enough men and material to launch an attack, the new

Right: The easy way and the hard way to search for mines. Royal Engineers clear an Axis minefield using acoustic detection gear on the Alamein Front, 28 August 1942, and Sappers search for mines under fire by prodding the ground in front of them with bayonets, on the very same day. No prizes for guessing which was the more popular task! (IWM E16226/E16232)

British commander aggressively set about raising the low morale of his troops, thus undermining the Axis commander's only real advantage in the battle to come.

For his attempt to break through the Allied defence line Rommel adopted a plan broadly similar to that used against the Gazala Line. Italian infantry divisions, stiffened by the 164th Infantry Division and other German units (Rommel no longer trusted these formations to perform without significant German cadres), were to launch limited attacks to pin

the 9th Australian, 1st South African and 5th Indian Divisions in position. Meanwhile the main striking force, comprising the 90th Light Division, the Italian Ariete Armoured and Trieste Motorised Divisions and the 15th and 21st Panzer Divisions, was to smash through the southern flank of the Allied line. Through surprise and rapidity of movement the Axis mechanised and motorised formations would strike deep into the Allied rear, disrupting their command and control mechanisms, sowing confusion and winning the psy-

Above: A driver takes cover behind the wheel of his truck during a bombardment near Mount Himeimat, 28 August 1942. (IWM E16092)

chological battle. The Allies' morale would collapse and they would be forced into a precipitate retreat. Unfortunately for Rommel his new opponent fully understood Blitzkrieg theory (he had been on the receiving end of it at Dunkirk) and he was not about to let the Panzerarmee commander run rings around him as

hadd been the case with previous 8th Army commanders.

The Battle of Alam Halfa began on the night of 30/31 August and began to go wrong almost immediately. The belts of mines which Rommel's forces had to penetrate were found to be far more elaborate than had been anticipated and many units were still struggling through them at dawn, by which time they should have been many miles further east. The slow-moving Axis formations provided easy targets of opportunity for marauding Allied aircraft , which cease-

lessly strafed and bombed the gaps in the minefields, causing heavy casualties, including the DAK commander, Nehring, who was badly wounded.

The British forces covering this sector of the line, the 4th Armoured Brigade and the 7th Motorised Brigade, did not attempt to halt the advance of the attacking Germans but withdrew before them in good order, picking off the leading panzers and half-tracks as they fell back. It was during one of these skirmishes that Georg von Bismarck, Commander of

Above: An Axis artillery shell explodes near a Bren Carrier on patrol near Mount Himeimat, 28 August 1942. (IWM E16094)

the 21st Panzer Division, was killed by a direct hit from a mortar bomb.

Rommel began to have serious doubts about the advisability of pushing on. Fortunately, however, at this point a desert sandstorm blew up which obscured his attacking troops from the air and allowed him to get back on schedule. When the storm subsided DAK and the Italian Ar-

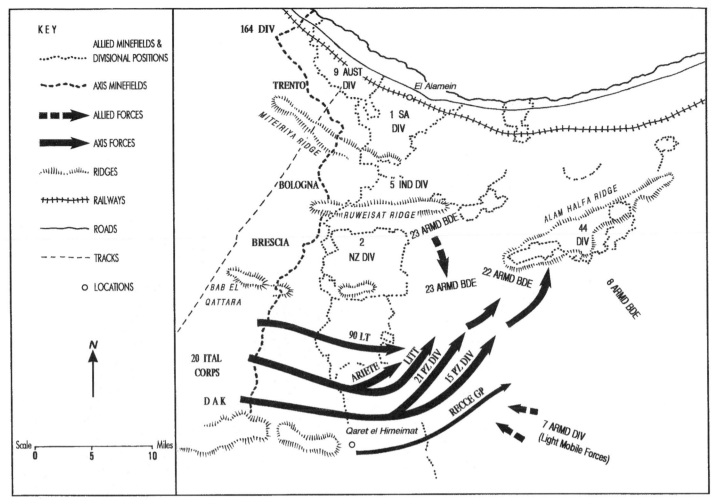

KEY

······· ALLIED MINEFIELDS & DIVISIONAL POSITIONS

– – – AXIS MINEFIELDS

▬▬▶ ALLIED FORCES

▬▬▶ AXIS FORCES

٬٬٬٬٬ RIDGES

+++++++ RAILWAYS

—— ROADS

– – – – TRACKS

○ LOCATIONS

N

Scale
0   5   10   Miles

moured Corps were well behind the Allied lines, some 15 miles south of the Alam Halfa Ridge.

At this point in battles fought in the past the British had always reacted to Axis thrusts, throwing in their armoured reserves in a series of headlong charges against DAK panzer and anti-tank gun screens. This Rommel fully expected them to do again. When the British tanks were defeated the Allied army's rear areas would be open for full exploitation.

However, this time Montgomery did not react as planned. In the fortnight before the battle he had reinvigorated the 8th Army, raised its morale and adjusted its strategy. He had drummed into his divisional and corps commanders that they must not lose their heads if they were outflanked: an enemy breakthrough did

not necessarily equate with an enemy victory (to be fair, Auchinleck had also realised this but had failed to transmit it to his generals). Throughout the Battle of Alam Halfa, the Allies were to hold the initiative: the Germans were unable to get within their enemy's decision-making cycle, and instead found themselves dancing to the British tune.

The role played by British armour in the battle illustrates the new tactics for the 8th Army. There were to be no massed counter-attacks at the point of the Axis breakthrough, as well-sited German anti-tank guns invariably broke up any armoured charge by the British. Strict instructions were issued that tanks were not to be allowed to get engaged in close conflict.

Montgomery allowed, even welcomed, the Axis advance deep into his

Above: The Battle of Alam Halfa, 31 August–2 September 1942.
Right, upper: Montgomery issues new instructions to a commander in the 22nd Armoured Brigade, 20 August 1942. (IWM E15790)
Right, lower: Crusaders of the 4th County of London Yeomanry behind Alam Halfa Ridge, 28 August 1942. (IWM E16277)

lines. Minefields and RAF ground attack aircraft caused favourable rates of attrition, whilst the withdrawal of the 4th Armoured Brigade and the 7th Motorised Brigade enticed DAK to continue its thrust.

When the expected British tank attacks failed to appear Rommel was faced with a dilemma. He could either push on to the east and risk becoming cut off by an Allied counterattack across his line of communication, or he could turn to the north and

assault Alam Halfa Ridge. From this the entire rear of the Allied positions could be surveyed, making them untenable. As Montgomery had foreseen, Rommel decided to attempt to capture the heights.

The ridge was defended by infantry and anti-tank guns of the 44th Infantry Division, and Grant tanks of the 22nd Armoured Brigade. Rommel's first attack was launched in the evening of 31 August, his new PzKpfw IV 'Specials' (panzers with high-velocity 75mm guns) in the van. The defending British troops were well dug in and had been told to expect exactly this kind of attack. The German assault failed.

The next day Rommel tried once again, but this time his attack was limited to the tanks of the 15th Panzer Division, due to a severe fuel shortage which left the 21st Panzer Division stranded in the open desert. This second attempt to capture the ridge was also defeated with heavy losses. In effect, the situation of previous battles had been reversed, the Germans wasting their strength in unsuccessful armoured assaults against a strong British defence line.

Rommel still hoped to achieve victory by luring the British tanks into pursuit of the retreating Axis forces and on to his defensive lines of 88mm guns and annihilating them. But Montgomery had strictly forbidden

Below: A near miss! A 6pdr anti-tank gun team under fire during the closing stages of the Alam Halfa engagement. (IWM E16406)

Above: The reality of tank-versus-tank combat: a disembowelled German panzer crewman lies next to his burnt-out PzKpfw III. Grim sights such as this were commonplace on the desert battlefield. This man met his end during the Alam Halfa battle when his tank was thrown against the Alam Halfa Ridge. (IWM E16495)

any armoured units to move from their defensive positions. Through adopting this rigid posture Montgomery forced Rommel to operate in an environment of his choosing.

In the morning of 2 September Rommel decided to retreat, but a shortage of fuel prevented any large-scale withdrawal during the day and DAK had to remain where it was, under ceaseless aerial bombardment and artillery attack. Some have argued that the time was now ripe for a counter-attack on the stranded panzer formations, which may well have achieved a crushing victory. Montgomery, however, was a cautious man. He did not trust his tank commanders to carry out a combined-arms assault that would not degenerate into a series of foolhardy

charges (and he was quite right not to do so). A substantial loss of British tanks might well have enabled Rommel to resume the offensive. It was better to settle for a limited victory than to take a gamble, which if it went wrong might see German troops in Alexandria. He had finally blunted the Axis' ability to launch any serious offensive. Now it was time to build up his reserves for an offensive of his own, an offensive that would not be characterised by ar-

moured shock action but by attritional 'crumbling', with infantry divisions playing a central role—an offensive that would begin with the Battle of El Alamein.

On 3 September 1942 Rommel's striking force was in full retreat to the west, leaving behind 50 knocked-out panzers, another 50 abandoned field and anti-tank guns and over 400 soft vehicles. With little ammunition, virtually no fuel and many of his best panzers destroyed, Rommel was in no position to contemplate any offensive action. All he could do was attempt to hold his ground and hope that Panzerarmee Afrika might significantly move up the priority list for reinforcements of men and material from German High Command. Unfortunately, with the summer offensive in Russia about to turn into the débâcle at Stalingrad, the Mediterranean theatre was to assume less, rather than more, importance in the eyes of the *Führer*.

The tide in North Africa had turned.

Below: : Germans captured during the closing stages of the Alam Halfa battle are put on display for the press, 6 September 1942. (IWM E16491)

INDEX

A

'Aberdeen', Operation, 110–14
Acroma, 98, 122
Agedabia, 16–17, 82–3, 88–9
Alamein, *see* El Alamein
Alam Halfa, 148, 151–2, 154–5
Alem Hamza, 98, 105–6
Antelat, 88–9
Aslagh Ridge, 108, 110, 112, 114–15
Auchinleck, General Sir Claude, 46–47, 50, 71, 73, 98, 112, 121, 131, 135, 144, 147, 149, 152
Australian units:
 Divisions: 7th, 28, 49; 9th, 11, 16, 28, 49, 139–40, 143–4, 146–7, 150
 Brigades: 18th, 28; 20th, 28; 24th, 28; 26th, 28, 143
 Regiments: 3rd Anti-Tank, 23

B

Bach, Reverend Major Wilhelm, 38–9, 84
Baldasarre, General Ettore, 14, 31, 97
Bardia, 35–7, 45, 62, 72–3, 75, 80, 84
Bastico, General Ettore, 47–8, 52–3, 83, 94–5
Belhamed, 66, 76, 122
Benghazi, 20, 82–3, 85, 92–4
Beresford-Peirse, General Sir Noel, 33, 37, 41, 43, 45–6
Bir el Chleta, 76
Bir el Gubi, 53, 57–9, 61, 66–8, 72, 81, 100, 104, 116
Bir el Harmat, 104, 112, 114, 117
Bir et Tamar, 112, 114
Bir Hacheim, 53, 97–8, 104, 106, 108, 115
Bir Lefa, 103
Bismarck, General Georg von, 88, 151
Boettcher, General Karl, 51
Briggs, Brigadier H. R., 94
Brink, General G. E., 49

British units:
 Armies:
  8th (creation of), 46
 Corps:
  X Corps, 132, 134–5, 137
  XIII Corps, 37, 49, 55, 61, 73, 97–8, 110–11, 132, 134–5, 137
  XXX Corps, 49, 54, 61–2, 73, 97–8, 110, 137
 Divisions:
  1st Armoured, 84–5, 88–91, 97–8, 100, 106, 131–2, 134–5, 146–7
  2nd Armoured, 11, 20, 23
  7th Armoured, 11, 36, 46, 49, 53–7, 65, 68–, 71–2, 77–8, 81–5, 97, 99–100, 110, 114, 137
  44th Infantry, 154
  50th Infantry, 97–8, 107, 116, 120, 131–5
  70th Infantry, 50, 55, 57, 64, 76–8, 85–6
 Brigades:
  2nd Armoured, 85, 90–1, 98–9, 103–4, 106, 108, 110, 118, 120
  3rd Armoured, 11, 20, 28
  4th Armoured, 37, 41, 49, 55, 57–8, 61, 65, 67, 69, 71, 75–7, 81–2, 99, 100, 104, 106, 110, 118, 120, 151
  7th Armoured, 34–5, 37–8, 40–5, 55, 57, 64, 69, 151
  22nd Armoured, 55, 57–9, 61, 65–6, 69, 76–7, 84, 98, 100, 103–4, 106, 108, 110, 112–15, 120, 137, 154
  23rd Armoured, 144–5
  1st Army Tank, 49, 55, 62, 65, 71, 74, 82, 84, 98, 103
  32nd Army Tank, 50, 55, 64, 71, 84, 98, 104, 110, 113–15, 126, 128
  7th Motorised, 99–100, 104, 116, 118, 122
  22nd Guards, 31, 34–5, 37, 39, 41–5, 49, 54, 61, 66, 68, 71, 80–2, 88
  69th Infantry, 98, 146–7

  150th Infantry, 98, 107–9
  151st Infantry, 98
  201st Guards, 88–90, 98–9, 116, 120, 126, 128
 Regiments:
  The Bays, 134
  King's Dragoon Guards, 14, 58, 60
  7th Hussars, 55, 65
  8th Hussars, 55, 67, 100
  11th Hussars, 31, 37, 48
  3rd County of London Yeomanry, 55, 100, 134
  4th County of London Yeomanry, 55, 100
  2nd Royal Gloucestershire Hussars, 55, 100, 103
  25th Field Regiment RA, 126
  72nd Field Regiment RA, 109
  3 Regiment RHA, 44
  4 Regiment RHA, 44
  104 Regiment RHA, 15, 23
 Battalions:
  1st RTR, 55
  2nd RTR, 35, 37, 39–41, 43, 55, 58
  3rd RTR, 55, 58, 60, 100
  4th RTR, 34, 37–9, 44, 55, 127
  5th RTR, 55
  6th RTR, 15–16, 35, 37, 39–41, 43, 55, 58, 63–4
  7th RTR, 37, 39, 41, 43–4, 55, 127
  8th RTR, 55
  42nd RTR, 55
  44th RTR, 55, 109
  1st The Buffs, 31
  2nd Cameron Highlanders, 37–9, 44
  3rd Coldstream Guards, 31, 127–8
  1st Duke of Cornwall's Light Infantry, 114
  1st Durham Light Infantry, 31, 35
  9th Durham Light Infantry, 134
  4th East Yorkshire, 109
  4th Green Howards, 109
  5th Green Howards, 109

1st King's Royal Rifle Corps, 35, 37, 44, 63, 66
2nd Rifle Brigade, 32, 34–5, 37, 44
2nd Scots Guards, 31, 43, 120
1st Sherwood Foresters, 128
1st Tower Hamlets Rifles, 14–15
1st Worcestershire, 120
Other units:
  1st Armoured Division Support Group, 85, 88–9
  7th Armoured Division Support Group, 44–5, 57, 64–6, 69
  E-Force, 60, 81–2
  Tobruk Garrison, 49–50
Buq Buq, 33, 45
Bush Artillery, 28

C

Campbell, Brigadier Jock, 44
Capuzzo, *see* Fort Capuzzo
Cauldron, The, 108–9, 112–14
Cavallero, General Ugo, 47, 83, 94
Churchill, Winston, 34–5, 46–7, 50, 121, 135
Coast Road, *see* Via Balbia
Creagh, General Michael, 37, 45
Crete, 36
Cruewell, General Ludwig, 47–8, 60, 64, 66, 68–9, 73, 95, 105, 107
Cunningham, General Sir Alan, 46–7, 55, 63, 73
Czech Battalion, The, 50

D

'Dash to the Wire', The, 70–6
Deir el Abyad, 137
Deir el Shein, 137
Derna, 24, 27, 36

E

Ed Duda, 76–8
Ehlert, Major, 21
El Adem, 29, 36, 98, 100, 104, 116–17, 120–3
El Agheila, 13–14
El Alamein, 135, 137, 140, 143–7
El Mireir, 144
Eluet et Tamar, 98, 120
Esebeck, General Freiherr von, 36

F

Fabris, Cornello, 20
Fisher, Brigadier, 147
Fletcher, Brigadier, 112–13
Fort Capuzzo, 34–7, 39–42, 44, 53, 75
French units:
  Brigades:
    1st Free French, 97–9, 104, 107, 115–16

2nd Free French, 116
Freyberg, General Bernard, 49, 78

G

Gabr Saleh, 53, 55–8, 61
Gambara, General Gastone, 48, 53, 94
Gambier-Parry, General, 11, 15, 23–5, 27
Gambut, 51, 54, 56, 66, 123
Gariboldi, General Italo, 9–10, 18, 47
Gatehouse, General Alec, 49, 58
Gazala, 81–2, 94, 96, 98
German units:
  Armies:
    Panzerarmee Afrika, 95
  Panzergruppen:
    Panzergruppe Afrika, 47–8, 83, 84
  Corps:
    Deutsches Afrika Korps (DAK) 9, 14, 47, 68, 71, 74, 97, 99, 103, 106, 108, 137–8, 146
  Divisions:
    15th Panzer, 9, 31, 36–7, 41–5, 47, 54, 56, 60–2, 64, 66–9, 73–8, 81, 83, 88–9, 91–2, 97, 100, 103, 105–6, 114–15, 117–18, 120, 122–3, 128, 132–3, 135, 138, 143, 145, 150, 154
    21st Panzer, 47–8, 51, 54, 56, 60–2, 64, 66, 68, 73–8, 81, 88–90, 92, 97, 103, 105, 109, 113–14, 117–18, 120–3, 128, 132–3, 135, 140, 143, 145, 150, 154
    5th Light, 9, 14, 16–18, 21, 27, 29, 37–45
    90th Light, 88, 95, 97, 100, 104–6, 109, 115, 117–18, 121, 123, 132–3, 135, 137, 150
    164th Infantry, 140, 150
    Afrika Division, 47, 60, 63, 68, 75, 77–8, 81–2
  Brigades:
    15th Rifle, 95, 98, 116
  Regiments:
    5th Panzer, 9, 27, 29, 41, 58, 68–9, 73–4, 78, 88, 109
    8th Panzer, 35, 37, 67, 69, 76, 88, 91, 106
    104th Infantry, 9, 37
    115th Infantry, 37
    155th Infantry, 64, 68, 78, 88
    200th Infantry, 147
    288th Infantry, 109
    361st Infantry, 47, 63–4, 68, 74, 95
    382nd Infantry, 140
    33rd Motorised Artillery, 37
    75th Motorised Artillery, 9
  Battalions:
    606th Anti-Aircraft, 9
    8th Machine Gun, 9, 16, 27, 29–30

39th Panzerjäger, 9
605th Panzerjäger, 9, 27
3rd Reconnaissance, 9, 16, 18, 27, 29, 56, 64, 68, 72, 73, 100, 122, 124, 143
33rd Reconnaissance, 56, 100, 122, 124, 143
580th Reconnaissance, 122, 124
Other units:
  Artillery Group 104, 51, 60, 63, 126, 140
  Group Cruewell, 95, 99, 105, 107
  Group Olbrich, 16, 21–5, 27
  Group Ponath, 23–4
  Group Schwerin, 17, 21, 23–5, 27
  Kampfgruppe Bach, 43–5, 84
  Kampfgruppe Herff, 32, 35
  Kampfgruppe Kiehl, 95–6, 98
  Kampfgruppe Marcks, 88–90, 92
  Kampfgruppe Menny, 124, 126
  1st Oasis Company, 40
Gioda, General Benvenuto, 96
Giorgis, General Fidele de, 53
Godwin-Austen, General Alfred, 49, 92, 94
Gott, General W. H. E., 34–5, 49, 57, 64–5, 68, 97, 111, 134, 149
Greece, 11

H

Hafid Ridge, 35, 37, 39–41
Halder, Field Marshal Franz, 13, 34
Halfaya Pass, 31–9, 41, 43–5, 53, 72–3, 75, 84
Halfway House, 32–4, 38, 53
Harding, Brigadier John, 24
'Hercules', Operation, 95, 129

I

Indian units:
  Divisions:
    4th Indian, 46, 49, 55, 61, 65, 73, 81–2, 85, 93–4
    5th Indian, 97, 110, 114, 131, 137, 150
    10th Indian, 131–2, 135
  Brigades:
    3rd Motorised, 11, 20, 23, 25, 27, 98–100
    29th Motorised, 60, 81, 98–9, 104, 116, 118, 122–3, 132
    5th Infantry, 143
    7th Infantry, 73–4, 94
    9th Infantry, 98, 110, 112, 113–15
    10th Infantry, 99, 110, 112, 114–15
    11th Infantry, 37–8, 41, 43–4, 73, 116, 124, 126, 128
    18th Infantry, 137
    20th Infantry, 116, 122

21st Infantry, 116
161st Infantry, 144
Regiments:
18th Cavalry, 28
3/12th Frontier Force Rifles, 122
2/5th Mahrattas, 37, 124, 126
1/6th Rajputana Rifles, 37
Other units:
Gleecol, 132–3
Leathercol, 132–3
Italian units:
Corps:
Corpo d'Armata di Manovra (CAM), 48
X Corps, 9, 14, 17, 21, 94–6, 107, 109
XX Corps, 88–9, 92, 94–5, 97, 99
XXI Corps, 48, 94–6, 116, 124, 132, 135
Divisions:
Ariete, 9, 14, 16, 20–1, 27, 29–31, 48, 53, 58–9, 68–9, 75, 77–8, 80–1, 88, 94, 97, 100, 103–4, 106, 108–12, 114, 117, 122, 128, 132, 135, 150
Bologna, 48, 54, 63–4, 72, 95
Brescia, 9, 14, 16, 18, 21, 23, 27, 29, 48, 54, 96, 143
Littorio, 95, 137
Pavia, 9, 14, 48, 54, 60, 63–4, 96, 107, 120
Sabratha, 96, 105–6, 139
Savona, 47, 53
Trento, 9, 14, 29, 30, 37, 48, 54, 96
Trieste, 48, 53, 72, 76–8, 80, 88, 97, 104, 106–7, 109, 117, 132, 135, 137, 140, 150
Regiments:
32nd Light Armour, 53
132nd Medium Armour, 53
7th Bersaglieri, 37
8th Bersaglieri, 27, 53
61st Infantry, 37
62nd Infantry, 37
2nd Motorised Artillery, 47
46th Artillery, 37
Battalions:
551st Anti-Tank, 37
3rd Bersaglieri Motorcycle, 25
Other units:
Group Fabris, 20–1, 23–4, 25, 27
Raggruppamento Esplorante (RECAM), 48, 72

J
Jalo, 82
Jebel Akhdar, 17, 20–1, 23, 91-92, 94
'Jock Columns', 32

K
Kesselring, Field Marshal Albrecht,

107–8, 130
King's Cross, 127–8
Kircheim, General Heinrich, 21, 31
Klopper, General H. B., 123, 127–8
Knightsbridge, 106, 114, 120

L
Lavarack, General J. D., 28

M
Maitland-Wilson, General Sir Henry, 10, 47
Malta, 84, 95, 129–30
Maraua, 94
Marcks, General Werner, 88, 123
Mechili, 20–1, 23, 25, 27, 36, 91–3
Mellenthin, Colonel F. W. von, 51, 139
Mersa el Brega, 14–15, 83–4, 94
Mersa Matruh, 130–5
Messervy, General Frank, 37, 43–5, 49, 90, 118
'Midsummer Night's Dream', Operation, 48–9
Minqa Qaim, 134
Montgomery, General Bernard Law, 149–50, 152, 154–5
Morshead, General L. J., 11, 28
Msus, 21, 23, 25, 90–3
Mugata, 9
Musaid, 34–5, 42

N
Naduret el Ghesceuasc, 117
Navarini, General Enea, 48, 96
Neame, General Philip, 11, 20, 24, 27
Nehring, General Walther, 97, 120, 151
Neumann-Sylkow, General Walther, 41–3, 45, 69, 82
New Zealand units:
Divisions:
2nd New Zealand, 49, 55, 57, 61–2, 65, 68, 71–2, 74, 76–8, 82, 85, 131–5, 143–4
Brigades:
4th New Zealand, 74, 138
5th New Zealand, 75–6
6th New Zealand, 68, 74, 137, 144
Norrie, General Willoughby M., 54, 97

O
O'Connor, General Richard, 10, 18, 20, 24
Olbrich, Colonel Friedrich, 16, 22, 30–1

P
Paulus, General Friedrich von, 34
Pilastrino Ridge, 126, 128
Point 175, 76, 78
Point 178, 64, 67–8

Point 186, 115
Point 206, 39
Point 208, 41
Point 209, 98, 115
Polish units:
Brigades:
1st Polish, 50
Ponath, Colonel, 23, 30
'Pop', Operation, 55, 63–4
Prittwitz und Gaffron, General Heinrich, 27–9

Q
Qarat el Abd, 139

R
Raml Ridge, 120
Ravenstein, General Johann von, 40, 45, 77
Reid, Brigadier, 123
Regima, 20
Retma Box, 100
Rigel Ridge, 103–5, 120
Ritchie, General Neil, 73, 84, 92–4, 97–8, 110, 112, 118, 121, 130–1
Rommel, Field Marshal Erwin, 9–10, 16–18, 21–3, 25, 27, 30–1, 41, 45, 47–8, 50–3, 60, 62, 66, 70–3, 75–7, 82–5, 88, 90–2, 94, 95, 98–9, 103, 105–6, 108–9, 116, 121–3, 130–1, 13–7, 150–5
Russell, Brigadier H. E., 41
Ruweisat Ridge, 137, 143–4

S
Saunnu, 89–0
Schwerin, Colonel Graf von, 17
Sidi Azeiz, 35, 37, 40, 62, 64–5, 76
Sidi Hamza, 131–2
Sidi Muftah, 106–9
Sidi Omar, 37–8, 42, 44, 53, 55, 61, 65, 73–4
Sidi Rezegh, 57, 59, 60–6, 68–9, 72, 74, 76–8, 122–3
Sidi Suleiman, 35, 44
Sidra Ridge, 108, 110–14
Sirte, 10
Sofafi, 48–9
Sollum, 34–7, 43, 53
South African units:
Divisions:
1st South African, 49, 53, 57, 61, 75, 78, 85, 97–8, 116, 120, 137, 150
2nd South African, 81, 84, 97, 98, 116, 126, 128
Brigades:
1st Infantry, 66, 68, 71, 77, 82, 98, 105, 137
2nd Infantry, 98, 137
3rd Infantry, 98, 143, 146–7

4th Infantry, 98, 126
5th Infantry, 66–70
6th Infantry, 98, 105, 116, 126
Regiments:
4th Armoured Car, 48–9, 59, 66, 99
6th Armoured Car, 60, 81
7th Armoured Car, 60, 81
Transvaal Scottish, 68
Streich, General Johannes, 14–15, 23, 30–1
Summerman, General Max, 47, 82

T
Taib el Esem, 75
Tell el Eisa, 144

Tengeder, 21
The Cauldron, *see* Cauldron, The
Tiger Convoy, 36
Tobruk, 27–31, 33, 35–7, 49–51, 55, 57, 63–4, 72, 76, 78, 80–1, 98, 117, 121–8
Totensonntag, 68
Tugun Emplacement, 64
Trigh Bir Hacheim, 106, 114
Trigh Capuzzo, 58, 60–1, 65, 68, 76, 103, 106–7
Trigh el Abd, 56, 58, 61, 75
Tripoli, 9, 84

U
'Ultra', 34

V
Vaerst, General Gustav von, 88
Via Balbia, 16, 18, 20, 60, 68, 72–3, 83, 88–9, 92, 94, 98

W
Wadi el Faregh, 88
Watkins, Brigadier H. R. B., 49
Wavell, General Sir Archibald, 12, 18, 20, 27, 34, 36, 45–7

Z
Zaafron, 76, 122